Recollections

of the

Storming

of the

Castle of Badajos

by the

Third Division, under the Command of Lieut. Gen. Sir Thomas Picton, G.C.B. on the 6th of April, 1812

RECOLLECTIONS

OF THE

STORMING

OF THE

CASTLE OF BADAJOS

BY THE

THIRD DIVISION, UNDER THE COMMAND OF LIEUT. GEN. SIR THOMAS PICTON, G.C.B. ON THE 6TH OF APRIL, 1812

BY

CAPTAIN MACCARTHY

The Spellmount Library of Military History

SPELLMOUNT
Staplehurst

British Library Cataloguing in Publication Data:
A catalogue record for this book is available
from the British Library

Copyright © Spellmount 2001
Introduction © Ian Fletcher 2001

ISBN 1-86227-131-3

First published in 1836

This edition first published in the UK in 2001
in
The Spellmount Library of Military History
by
Spellmount Limited
The Old Rectory
Staplehurst
Kent TN12 0AZ
United Kingdom

Tel: 01580 893730
Fax: 01580 893731
E-mail: enquiries@spellmount.com
Website: www.spellmount.com

1 3 5 7 9 8 6 4 2

Printed in Great Britain by
T.J. International Ltd
Padstow, Cornwall

AN INTRODUCTION
By Ian Fletcher

The night of 6 April 1812 remains one of the most momentous in the long, bloody and distinguished history of the British Army. After three weeks of toiling in the rain and mud in the trenches in front of the Spanish fortress of Badajoz, Wellington's infantry hurled themselves at the massive walls and despite fierce French resistance that accounted for hundreds of their number, they emerged victorious.

It was a remarkable feat, achieved against the odds, and was one that moved their commander-in-chief, Lord Wellington, never one to eulogise, to pay his men a fine tribute. 'The storming of Badajoz', he wrote, 'affords as strong an instance of the gallantry of the British soldier as has ever been displayed, but I sincerely hope I shall never be the instrument of putting them to such a test as that to which they were put last night.' It was, however, not the first time his men had been asked to fling themselves at the walls of a Spanish fortress, nor would it be the last, but never had so much been asked of them than at Badajoz.

Captain James MacCarthy, of the 50th (West Kent) Regiment – they had yet to be given the Royal prefix – was the assistant engineer attached to Sir Thomas Picton's 3rd Division. His splendid book, *Recollections of the Storming of the Castle of Badajos*, recalls that terrible night when he guided the 3rd Division to the assault, during which he was severely wounded. It is a short but wonderfully descriptive work, full of detail and graphic anecdotes, both horrific and humorous alike. This book, the latest in the acclaimed Spellmount Library of Military History, is a reprint of the second edition of MacCarthy's book, originally published in 1836.

The year 1812 had begun in a blaze of glory for Wellington when, on the cold and frosty night of 19 January, his men snatched the Spanish fortress town of Ciudad Rodrigo from the French. Winter was a time when, traditionally, armies went into cantonments to recover from the year's campaigning. But as New Year's Day approached Wellington, the supposed 'cautious general', was planning an audacious attack on the old Moorish town which, if successful, would give him command of the northern corridor between Spain and Portugal.

After just nine days of open trenches Wellington sent in the 3rd and Light Divisions to assault the walls in two places where breaches had been made by the guns of the Royal Artillery. The resistance put up by the French, under General Barrie, was brief, and cost the lives of two British major-generals, Robert 'Black Bob' Craufurd and Henry Mackinnon. The Light Division passed relatively easily through the Lesser Breach whilst the 3rd Division successfully stormed the Greater Breach, but not before a huge explosion had sent about two hundred of its number hurtling into the sky.

Once inside, the successful stormers dispersed for a brief period while they scoured the houses and shops for drink, food and plunder. Many gathered in the Plaza Mayor and gave vent to their feelings by firing upon the buildings that surrounded it, whilst others set fire to some houses. The period of disorder was brutal, if brief, but the significance of the event should not be overlooked, for it gave the British soldiers a taste of what they could expect and enjoy – if they survived – when they attacked Badajoz, which they knew would be next on Wellington's Spanish wish list.

The capture of Ciudad Rodrigo gave Wellington command of the northern corridor between Spain and Portugal and once this was in his possession he turned his attention to Badajoz, which controlled the southern corridor. The capture of Ciudad Rodrigo came as a great shock to the French, whose winter hibernation had just begun. But if they thought this was the end of Wellington's 'out of season' operations, they were sadly mistaken, for even while his men began repairing the walls of Ciudad Rodrigo, others were slipping away to the south in readiness for the attack on Badajoz

The fortress of Badajoz is a mighty one and is situated on the southern bank of the Guadiana river. Any traffic between Spain and Portugal had to proceed via the town, hence its importance. Any army commander wishing to move either east or west could not even contemplate such a move without possession of the place for if it were left in the hands of the enemy, communications and supply lines would be severely compromised.

When Wellington's men approached Badajoz on 16 March 1812 they did so with the bitter memory of the previous year's failure to take the place etched in their minds. In June 1811, British and Portuguese soldiers had been cut down during two attempts to storm Fort San Christobal, an outwork situated on the northern bank of the Guadiana, possession of which would possibly have forced the French governor of Badajoz, General Armand Phillipon, to surrender the town. But it was not to be. The defenders of Fort San Christobal held out and Wellington was forced to withdraw.

In March 1812 Wellington approached Badajoz with renewed optimism, borne of the success at Ciudad Rodrigo. This optimism was well founded but the siege was far from satisfactory. Indeed, the siege operations in the Peninsula were the most unhappy aspect of what was otherwise a very successful campaign. There was a lack of siege tools, heavy guns were at a premium, and with no trained sappers or miners in Wellington's army, the digging devolved upon the ordinary line infantry who positively loathed the business.

Siege warfare was a science. First of all, engineers had to carry out a thorough reconnaissance of the target in order to identify weak points. When this had been done and the point of attack selected, plans would be drawn up for the construction of trenches, or parallels as they were known, after which batteries were constructed. Then, once the batteries had been armed, the guns would open fire on the selected targets. Even then it was simply a case of blasting away at the walls, for the gunners were trained to fire at the foot of the walls in order to bring the wall tumbling into the ditch. This, in theory, would create a kind of ramp, up which the storming columns would attack. If the breaches were not large enough or if the defences had not been cleared of all obstacles, the consequences for the attacking troops could be dire. Despite the efforts of both engineers and artillery, the siege degenerated into what Wellington later called 'sheer bludgeon work.'

The siege itself was marked by dreadful weather. Heavy rained rendered the effective construction of protective parallels almost impossible. The spoil refused to pile up and instead ran back in streams into the foot of the trench. Wellington's situation was not helped either by the fact that he was up against a resourceful and very active opponent. Indeed, Phillipon was the epitome of an aggressive defender, always encouraging his men, leading sorties and ensuring that the spoil and rubbish which accumulated at the foot of the walls were cleared away each night.

Nevertheless, by the evening of 5 April two large breaches, in the Santa Maria and Trinidad bastions, had been blasted and arrangements made for the assault later that same night. However, whether he was uncertain as to the practicability of the breaches or whether he merely wished to facilitate the path for his stormers, Wellington postponed the attack until a third breach had been made, this time in the curtain wall between the two breached bastions. Throughout the next day, 6 April, Wellington's gunners blasted away at the curtain wall with their huge 24-pounder guns, until by nightfall a third breach had been made. Wellington then issued orders for the attack to take place at nine o'clock that same night.

The attack on the breaches was to be made by the 4th and Light Divisions, with diversionary attacks being made by the 3rd Division, at the Castle, and by the 5th Division, at the San Vicente bastion, in the north-west corner of the city. These latter two attacks were to be made by escalade, that is to say, with ladders.

Although James MacCarthy was no engineer, he volunteered for service in the engineers' department for the duration of the siege. His own regiment, the 50th, formed part of Rowland Hill's 2nd Division, which played no part in the actual siege. MacCarthy's account of the storming of Badajoz recalls the 3rd Division's attack on the Castle, an attack made by escalade in the face of tremendous French opposition. MacCarthy, in fact, was lucky to get to the Castle, for he was almost cut down by a furious Sir Thomas Picton who, upon hearing the main attacks at the breaches beginning, and sensing that MacCarthy was lost, threatened to cut him down. Ironically, Picton was wounded soon afterwards and thus took no further part in the storming, contrary to numerous contemporary pictures which have him standing on top of the ramparts of the castle.

Initially, few men survived long enough at the top of the walls of the Castle to even shout about it, let alone establish a foothold. The long ladders were filled from top to bottom with eager British soldiers, all of whom were desperate to get inside the city where plunder and pillage awaited them. But the French made them fight for it. With the attack at the breaches floundering in the bloodiest possible style, the success of the two diversionary attacks suddenly became absolutely essential. The British troops stood aghast at the foot of the walls, despairing of ever gaining entry, but, just when all seemed lost, Henry Ridge, of the 5th Foot, gained a foothold on the walls. Another officer followed and suddenly, and miraculously, a group of British soldiers stood defiantly upon the walls of Badajoz. Others followed and soon hundreds were pouring over into the Castle enclosure. Sadly, Henry Ridge was not among them for he was mortally wounded whilst still on the ramparts.

With the success of the attack by the 3rd Division, Badajoz can be said to have been won. The 5th Division, no less heroic, had achieved its objective and had scaled the walls of the San Vicente bastion. With the two divisions advancing in rear of the French defenders at the breaches, all opposition slacked off and the city was won. The 4th and Light Divisions made over forty separate attacks on the breaches but not one succeeded. Indeed, such were the formidable barriers placed in their way, they were hard pressed to gain entry even in daylight the next morning, and with the French gone.

Some 3,500 casualties were sustained during the assault, mainly at the breaches. It was a savage price to pay, and it is little wonder that Wellington broke down and wept the next morning when he inspected the breaches and saw the shattered remains of two of his finest divisions. Amongst the wounded was MacCarthy himself, which meant that he was not present throughout the following three days of debauchery that followed the storming of Badajoz. Convention of the day dictated that, should a breach be deemed practicable, the garrison would be summoned to surrender and be allowed to march out with honour. Unfortunately, Napoleon decreed that none of his garrison commanders was to surrender a town without first having sustained at least one assault. This, however, meant that the stormers would incur casualties that they considered unnecessary. Thus, in their eyes, the garrison waived all rights to mercy. The strange thing was, that when Wellington's men broke into the town, they took out their anger not on the French but on the inhabitants of the town and their property. MacCarthy mentions rather quaintly that as a reward for their labours during the siege the men, once inside, would 'rummage the town,' which is putting it mildly. In fact, they were out of control for a full three days before they began to return to their camps.

The sacking of Badajoz was one of the most shameful deeds ever committed by soldiers of the British Army, but who could blame them? Wellington certainly did not. Indeed, one suspects that he felt partly responsible for the catastrophe in the breaches. He later wrote in a letter that had he put the garrison of Ciudad Rodrigo to the sword he would have spared the flower of his army at Badajoz. 'I say this to show that the slaughtering of a garrison is not a useless effusion of blood,' Wellington added chillingly. Unfortunately for the British stormers at Badajoz he spared the garrison of Ciudad Rodrigo and thus the defenders of the former fortress became encouraged to fight on.

Sadly, the harsh lessons of Ciudad Rodrigo and Badajoz were not absorbed by Wellington's army, for the whole process was to be repeated at San Sebastian in 1813, a siege with an equally shocking aftermath. When the town fell on 31 August 1813 it was sacked with a savagery that matched that of Badajoz but was made worse by a fire that engulfed most of the town. Strangely enough, most diarists chose not to go into too much detail, simply writing that the sacking was either as bad, or worse, than at Badajoz. One wonders whether they had simply exhausted themselves in writing of Badajoz and kept the afterrnath of San Sebastian short and simple.

Eye-witness accounts of the storming of Badajoz are plentiful enough, as befits the momentous if terrible event. MacCarthy's account, written twenty-four years later, is one of the rarer ones. The book is not the usual lengthy memoir but is, rather, an account of the siege and storming of Badajoz only, although two pieces at the end of the book recall the storming of Fort Napoleon at Almaraz, in which the 50th played a leading role, and the Battle of Corunna, in which the regiment fought also. It is MacCarthy's account of Badajoz, however, that is the most valuable, not least for the fact that is was MacCarthy who guided the 3rd Division to its attack on the castle. The emphasis is, naturally enough, on the 3rd Division, and on Sir Thomas Picton, for whom MacCarthy obviously had a great deal of admiration, and who died a hero's death at Waterloo in June 1815. Picton's two sisters, in fact, appear on the list of subscribers. Here, then, is MacCarthy's tale of the storming of Badajoz and of his own part in the action, which he modestly describes as being 'only actions of duty.'

Ian Fletcher
Rochester 2001

RECOLLECTIONS

OF

THE STORMING OF THE CASTLE

OF

BADAJOS;

BY THE

THIRD DIVISION, UNDER THE COMMAND OF

LIEUT. GEN. SIR THOMAS PICTON, G.C.B.

ON THE 6th OF APRIL, 1812.

A PERSONAL NARRATIVE,

BY CAPTAIN MAC CARTHY, LATE OF THE 50TH REGIMENT,

ASSISTANT ENGINEER, 3rd DIVISION.

TO WHICH ARE ADDED MEMOIRS OF THE

STORMING OF FORT NAPOLEON, ALMAREZ;

AND OF

THE BATTLE OF CORUNNA.

SECOND EDITION.

LONDON:

PUBLISHED BY W. CLOWES AND SONS, CHARING CROSS.

ERRATA.—Page 47 line 7, for *preceding* read *previous to*.

ADDRESS.

HAVING been informed by a friend, that he had read " The Memoirs of Sir Thomas Picton," in which my name was mentioned; and that a *private* letter of mine to Sir Thomas was inserted in the appendix! I felt considerable regret that I was not apprised, nor aware, of such an intention previously to the appearance of the work, as I *might* have corresponded — *ingenuously*—with the author; which, however — besides the inducements herein mentioned—impel me to narrate in the following pages, relative occurrences interesting and authentic—not be fore published.

Jan. 1st, 1836.

NOTE.

THIS is not intended as a progressive account of the scientific operations of the Siege of Badajos; nor to publish—vauntingly —my own deeds, which, however arduous, were only actions of duty; but, is designed to supply the vast vacuum in the History of that Siege.

M.

LIST OF SUBSCRIBERS.

His Grace The Duke of Marlborough, (2 copies)

General The Rt. Hon. Lord Hill, G.C.B., G.C.H.,
 K.C., Commanding-in-chief

Lt.-General The Rt. Hon. Sir Hussey Vivian, Bart.,
 K.C.B., G.C.H. Master-Gen. of the Ordnance

Lt.-General The Hon. Sir Charles Colville, G.C.B.
 G.C.H.

Lt.-General The Rt. Hon. Lord Howard of Effingham,
 G.C.B.

Lt.-General The Rt. Hon. Sir George Murray,G.C.B.
 G.C.H.

Lt.-General The Rt. Hon. Sir James Kempt, G.C.B.,
 G.C.H.

Lt.-General Sir George T. Walker, Bart., G.C.B.

Lt.-General Sir William Hutchinson, K.C.B.

M.-General The Rt. Hon. Lord Fitz-Roy Somerset,
 K.C.B.

Col. The Rt. Hon. The Earl of Munster, A.D.C. to
 the King

The Rt. Hon. Lord John Spencer Churchill

Col. Arnold, K.H., Royal Eng., A.D.C. to the King

Lt.-Colonel Cockburn, Royal Artillery

Lt.-Colonel Thorn, Asst. Q.M. General

Capt. Boxer, R.N., Dover

Major Maling, A.M. Sec. to Com.-in-chief, at the
 Horse Guards

Major Garvock, Adjutant-general's Office

Captain Roche Meade, K.H., 21st regt. ditto.

Lt.-Colonel Drummond, Heath, Oxford

Captain Stopford, Royal Artillery

Captain Warde,   ditto

Lieut. Jephson, (2 copies) ditto

Lieut. Hotham, Royal Engineers

Capt. Dean, 5th regiment Fusiliers

Capt. King,   ditto

M.-General The Rt. Hon. Sir H. Hardinge, K. C. B.

Mrs. (Col.) Williams,
Mrs. Stokes } Sisters of Sir Thos. Picton

Colonel Faunce, C. B.—I.F.O. Bristol, A.D.C. to the
    King

Lt.-Colonel Digby Mackworth, K. H. — A. D. C. to
    Lord Hill

Capt. Warde, Royal Artillery, (2nd copy)

Lieut. Massey Dawson, 5th regiment Fusiliers

The Rev. R. B. De Chair, Shepherd's Well

The Rev. Frederick De Chair, East Langdon

Thomas Warner, Esq. Manchester

Mr. R. Page, Dover

Thomas Martin, Esq. M.P. Ballinaherd Castle.

PREFACE.

MANY have written, and many others may write on the same subject, but each in a different theme; because all tell their own story their own way, according to their estimation of the events, on which their conclusions were founded, as exemplified in this narrative; and, there are those, who by compilation assume the character of narrators of what themselves, otherwise, are totally unacquainted with; but the following pages *invite* the recognition of the SURVIVORS of the Siege of Badajos, to FACTS of importance to THEM, interesting to all others, HONOURABLE TO THE BRITISH ARMY,— and, EVERLASTING IN THE PAGE OF HISTORY!

The sublime is truth—and therefore the

narrator's pen (like the magnetic-needle) points at accuracy—though he may sometimes have said too little, from intervening circumstances of those NOT within his own observation, where more was required, or expected; and sometimes too much (of himself perhaps) where less would have sufficed. He has also taken the liberty of expressing a few moral reflections on pathetic occurrences, as they arose in his mind.

The continued, unimpaired, and brilliant success of the British arms by sea and land, amidst myriads of obstacles (physical and political) supported by mighty power, is the best proof of the perfection of those establishments! And, on the perusal of the following pages subjects will be found illustrative, unalloyed by flattery or comment; but, creating emulation in the breasts of future warriors—for, men are taught by precedent as well as precept.

The narrator begs to observe, that, in what has been published on the Siege of Badajos,

insufficiency is experienced relative to the
Storming of the Castle, which the following
develops and records; and though small in
quantity, and concise as is the period this describes, it is hoped that it will be considered
extensive in quality : and, notwithstanding it
has been admitted that the capture of the
Fortress of Badajos was attained by the escalade of its Castle, it is not *fully* known
how that event occurred—but the

> " Mysterious keeper of the key
> —— Opes the gate of memory !"

And,

> The warrior from strife retired,
> By mem'ry his soul's inspired;
> And turns to deeds of glory done,
> Dangers escap'd, and battles won.

Ruminations and references, therefore, occupied the mind, in selecting interesting
occurrences to refresh the narrator's memory
—en rêverie—in arranging his " Recollections" of the victorious escalade.

The brilliant conquest of the FORT NA-
POLEON, by half a brigade of Lord Hill's
Division, so worthy of record, as ONE OF
THE GREAT ACHIEVEMENTS OF THE BRI-
TISH ARMY, is little known beyond the offi-
cial dispatch of the day. But (being confined at Badajos with his wound) at that
time, the narrator obtained from brother
officers (wounded at Almarez) sojourning with
him, and subsequently, from regimental ar-
chives and legends, the most interesting
particulars, which are here subjoined.

At CORUNNA likewise, (where the narrator
was also wounded) the first brigade of General
Moore's army, under Lord William Bentinck,
sustained the powerful attack of the enemy:
this has been only *slightly* noticed in the
several publications, occasioned by the difficulty of accurate information being gleaned
from the vague reports of the scattered
individuals; but, the narrator is enabled to
add hereto his perfect recollection of that
portion of THE BATTLE OF CORUNNA.

RECOLLECTIONS

OF

STORMING THE CASTLE

OF

BADAJOS.

In presenting to the public biographical illustrations of Lieut. General Sir Thomas Picton, Lieut. General The Right Hon. Sir James Kempt, Major General The Right Hon. Lord Fitz-Roy Somerset, and others, it is hoped, that possessing several particulars—not made known—which redound to the honour of the gallant Generals, and communicating those FACTS as they occurred in detail, will be acceptable.

The storming of Badajos is an important subject in the page of history: the conquest of the Castle, one of the most arduous and brilliant achievements thereof was accomplished by General Picton's Division—on a plan proposed by himself—; and illumines, for ever, his martial fame.

Regard for the memory of General Picton; for the honour and renown of his gallant Division; and, having had the honour—as Assistant-Engineer—of conducting that Division, are inducements to avail myself of this, much-desired, opportunity of explaining my strongly-impressed recollections of that bold and successful enterprise — the escalade of the Castle of Badajos.——

Lieut. General Sir Thomas Picton's acute ideas, and accurate conception—his presence of mind, and strength of mind, adapted him for enterprize—however perilous;—which, with his martial spirit, always ensured success.

He naturally watched the progress of the Siege of Badajos, and contemplating the means of a termination the most speedy and certain, ran his ideas around the extensive and powerfully defended Fortress, and felt convinced that, as an escalade of the Castle was not likely to be expected by the besieged, THERE was the most accessible point.

Having arranged in his own mind, the escalade, and approaches to the several other objects of attack, and the distribution of the troops, so as to arrest the destructive defences the enemy had prepared against the breaches, and with his reserve to seize the Castle, the General presented those ideas when called upon.

This arduous task was confided to him, and he led his Division to the attack with the utmost confidence: and though wounded early, he had so previously instructed the Brigades, that notwithstanding the enemy on finding the Castle attacked, augmented its defenders and resorted to extraordinary destructives, General Picton's Division prevail-

ed, and exultingly possessed the Castle, en-
abling the other Divisions of the Army to
enter the town.

Thus, it will be shown, was the conquest
of the " Impregnable* Fortress of Badajos,"
attained!!!

I beg the indulgence of refreshing my
memory, by commencing with the era of
my joining the Besieging-Army, and noting
remarkable circumstances during the Siege,
to bring perfectly to my remembrance, in
detail, the escalade and extraordinary events
connected therewith, which fell to the lot
of an individual.

To describe the heroism of our soldiers in
the Siege, would be impossible; and unnecessary to say more than, that they possessed
British hearts : and, of those destined for the
escalade of the Castle (within my observa-
tions) every individual—officers and men—
vied with each other in intrepidity, so
devotedly, as to render it difficult to distin-
guish the BRAVEST *of the* BRAVE!

* So named by the French.

Being desirous of participating in the Siege of Badajos (on a scale so extensive) and my regiment, in General Hill's Division, then in Albuquerque, I wrote a letter to Colonel Stewart, 50th regiment, soliciting permission to go to the Siege " on the forlorn-hope duty, should no preferable person be appointed."—It is said, that those who do *only* their duty do WELL; but, that those who volunteer, *do more*.—Three days afterward, my regiment having marched to Merida, general orders were received permitting a portion of officers to serve at the Siege of Badajos as Assistant-Engineers, and requesting their names. I immediately embraced this opportunity, as affording the means of obtaining, by extraordinary exertion, the soldier's reward—approbation and promotion— and sent in my name; as did Captain Montgomery, who had lately rejoined from the Military College, and was anxious to add practice to theory.

The Division was ordered to Talavera del

Real, and Captain Montgomery and myself to proceed forthwith to Badajos.

On entering the encampment on the Tala-vera side, and enquiring for the Engineers' camp (which was four miles off) we were saluted by many in the regiments we passed through, with the consoling remark (iron-ically) of, " here come some more ' Fire-eaters;' " anticipating, I presume, that we were volunteers devoted to the severe duty of Assistant-Engineers.

On arrival late in the day in the Engineers' camp, which was the nighest to the trenches, we reported ourselves to Majors Burgoyne and Squiers (Colonel Fletcher being confined to his pallet by a severe wound): to THEM I expressed my object, and wishes to be employed on extraordinary occasions beyond the usual tour of duty: which I afterwards took an opportunity of repeating to Colonel Fletcher in his tent. I was attached to the 2d Brigade in the charge of Captain——R.E.

The first parallel was commenced, and

carried on with great perseverance; and all the batteries which were (temporarily) constructed to protect the working parties, and assail the besieged, were successively dismantled, as the progress of the approaches rendered them unnecessary; previously to which, several of the guns and magazines were injured by the enemy, two or three were dismounted, and in another, a twenty-four-pound shot entered the muzzle of the gun so precisely, as to split it equally on both sides (like the spout of a tea-kettle) as far as the band, and remained there, without disturbing the gun in its position: but, notwithstanding the heavy rains inundated the trenches and decomposed every shovelfull of earth as it was thrown up, so that the embankments could not retain their consistency, the works were continued with extraordinary vigour; and the Engineer department became very severe.

The Engineers were on duty in the trenches eight hours, and off four hours, alternately. The working-parties were relieved every six hours—and the guard in the trenches every twelve hours.

Captain ——, R. E. was *a most singular* character; who, when marking out the ground for No. 7, great breaching battery, very near the wall, which was always lined with French soldiers waiting for objects to fire at, he used to challenge them to prove the perfection of their marksmen, by lifting up the skirts of his coat in defiance, several times in the course of his survey; and then deliberately measuring the ground by prescribed paces, driving stakes, setting spades, &c.; and, when he had finished his task, make his "congé" by again lifting the skirts of his coat and taking off his hat, amidst their ineffectual firing at him, although a soldier of our working party close to the captain, was struck, in the act of stooping, by a ball on the pouch-belt where it crosses the bayonet-belt behind. The man screamed with agony, and the French laughed; but on examining him, he was found only to have been hurt by the concussion, both belts and the coat having been cut through as if slit with a penknife, without touching his skin.

Whilst attending the construction of No. 7 battery, I took an opportunity of stepping into Fort Picurina, on the fourth day after the capture of it—the storming of which by "The Brave General Kempt," with the 3d Division, was one of the most brilliant exploits of the Peninsular Army. It was a redoubt strongly armed, and surrounded by a deep trench in which were fixed very large earthen-vessels* filled with combustibles, and furnished above them with bundles of hemp, pitch, &c.; each suspended from the end of a long stake firmly planted in the parapet, and leaned outwards to give light when ignited, and to drip fire into those pots below and cause explosion: the counterscarp was also undermined. This Fort was connected with the Town by a bridge of planks on trestles, over the inundation, the half of which was demolished, and many French soldiers drowned in their

* Oil Jars.

panic to regain the Town, and their bodies
left floating in the water: several others were
left dead in the fosse, but only one British
soldier, with green facings. The side of the
Fort next the bridge was barricaded with
strong palisades, in which was a massive
gate, and, being defended by the Fortress,
was considered secure; but, so determined
and precipitate was the attack, that the enemy had not time to explode the mines. The
defence was sanguinary till overpowered by
our gallant fellows, and the enemy fled in
confusion.—Thus was the capture of Fort
Picurina.—I entered by the gate (which was
broken) to contemplate the attack and defence, several French soldiers firing at me as
soon as I appeared; all was in a state of
demolition. A sergeant's guard, consisting
of various men of a British Brigade, had
charge of the place, and were lolling and
laying about; and near them a French soldier laid stretched on his back, his face
broiling in the sun. I supposed him dead.
—He was without clothes, except a French

great coat which was spread upon him.
Seeing his right hand upon his face, I approached him—he was alive—and holding
his nose with his thumb and fingers. On
hearing me speak to the sergeant he dropped his hand upon his breast: his mouth
was parched and gasping. I took hold of
his hand—his pulse seemed regular but
strong. I applied to the guard for water,—
they had none. I resolved to assist him; but
at this moment was recalled to the working men by the arrival of Major Squires, R.E.
—involuntarily expressing to the guard my
sympathy; and, my regret at the neglect of
those whose *duty* it was to administer assistance in such cases. The guard seemed
indifferent to the man. I had not time,
then, to ascertain what injuries he had received, and determined to return; which I
did in about two hours, and was surprised
at not finding the man there. The guard
had been relieved, and the new guard knew
nothing of the circumstance. I examined the
ground, trench, and inundation, supposing

B

him to have expired and been thrown over,
or perhaps buried; and made every enquiry
but could never gain any information relative
to him. This must appear to the reader as
extraordinary as to myself—that, a fellow-
creature should have remained on the ground
in the centre of the Fort severely wounded
four days without assistance—or sustenance;
and can only be ascribed to the possibility
of his having been " passed by on the other
side," by those who supposed him dead—
and I lament, to this moment, that, having
found him alive, I had neither " oil nor
wine" to administer unto him.

The day after the above occurrence, a
field-officer of the guard in this part, being desirous of examining the town, placed
(as was usual) his hat at some distance from
himself on the bank, to allure the attention
of the French soldiers, who with their muskets presented on their wall, were watching
opportunities to fire at individuals. This
officer placed his spy-glass on the bank and
screened it with a shovel; but, the instant

he applied his eye to the glass, a shot from the enemy pierced his forehead, and he fell dead.——Numerous were the accidents and occurrences in the trenches, and some of them very extraordinary.

The enemy always kept a guard of several soldiers in the square tower of the church, in Badajos, which had extensive lattices on each side, overlooking the trenches, and by climbing upon the cross-beams, they watched the besiegers, and gave notice when the working parties, or the guard, were being relieved; which, at first, by the reliefs arriving in the works, and the relieved departing, both at the same time, (consisting of between two and three thousand men,) excessively crowded the trenches, among whom the enemy instantly opened a tremendous fire of shot and shell, and caused great destruction. In consequence, the reliefs were ordered not to enter until all those to be relieved had quitted the trenches. Nevertheless, whenever either the working parties or the guard were passing, or any considerable number of men proceeding in the trenches, the enemy, by the information of the watchmen on the church, threw shot and shell with effect. I pointed out to an artillery officer, the fellows in their white trousers, swinging their legs as they sat in the tower, and suggested a shot at them from a twenty-four pounder his men were working, but—" He had no orders."

The enemy's artillery was directed with great precision. When breaking ground for No. 10 battery we were much annoyed, soon after day-light, by several shots and shells thrown into the work, two of which were remarkable :—The working-party was retiring to make room for the relief, and the last man stood by my side waiting his turn to pass out, (alternately,) and hesitating to allow me to precede him, I desired him to pass, as I was not going; at that instant, a cannon shot (lobbed, according to the soldiers' phrase,) fell upon him, and tore out his intestines entire, from his right breast to his left hip, and they hung against his thighs and legs as an apron—instantly he lost his balance and fell. I called a corporal and two men of his regiment to return and bury him, and to report to his commanding officer the circumstance. Having to remain for the succeeding workmen a considerable time before they could arrive, I fixed a shovel in the bank near the same spot, and sat down; and, with two men of the corps of Artificers, were watching the fall of numerous shells thrown at the work, when one of the men said, " A shell is coming here, Sir." I looked up, and beheld it approaching me like a cricket-ball to be caught; it travelled so rapidly, that we had only time to run a few paces, and crouch, when it entered the spot on which I had been sitting, and exploding, destroyed all our night's work.

When superintending the opening of the second parallel, about midnight, the enemy, attracted by the sound of the mattocks and spades, directed a constant fire of their musketry upon the working party, and so considerably interrupted the men, that they were

obliged to work upon their hands and knees;
but, two ingeniously cautious fellows, (taking
advantage of the engineer's attention to other
parts of the work) dug each a pit of about
two yards square, and five feet deep, for
themselves to repose in, until routed by the
return of the engineer with the field-officer,
who, by the bye, finding these " snug quar-
ters," took possession, and obliged the men
to cut down the partition they had left between the two pits, and continue the trench;
(the Portuguese soldiers certainly worked well
and bravely, in competition with the British) ;
during which the attention was attracted by
the naked body of a dead man, (a soldier,)
about twenty paces distant, which, on ex-
amination, appeared to have been buried—
hastily—in a very shallow grave, much too
short; and, that he had revived and strug-
gled out of it, but expired upon the surface
in a writhing position; his body was heaved
upwards, supported by his elbows over the
sides of the grave, his head bent backwards
over one end, and his legs drawn up and

resting with his heels over the other end, and quite stiff. He was like a large stool on four legs (viz. head, elbows, and heels) placed over a hole much smaller than itself. A sudden occurrence prevented his being again interred, and he was left to dissolve upon the earth, in the due course of nature, as were numerous brother sufferers in warfare, like all things which have " run their course,"—men or trees,—and, as an ingredient in the combination of particles for future structures.

No. 7 battery was completed with twelve twenty-four pounders, and commenced its tremendous fire about six o'clock in the morning of the 31st of March, which the enemy answered with showers of shot and shells so effectually as to explode the magazine three hours afterwards; and by noon a considerable part of the battery was in ruins. An officer of artillery from this battery met Captain ———*, myself, and two artificers, in the trenches, and

* Page 16.

told the Captain that he was desired by the officer commanding in No. 7 battery to tell him to inform Colonel Fletcher, that the battery was so much damaged the men could not stand to their guns; and to request that a party might be sent immediately to repair it. The captain seemed displeased, and replied he could not spare time, and that the artillery officer should carry his message himself. The officer repeated, that he was ordered to deliver this message to the first engineer he met. Captain ———— was sent the next day to the Invalid-Depôt at Elvas, on account of an injury he received in his head at the Siege of Rodrigo. I was proceeding afterwards in the trenches,* and met two artillery-men carrying, in a blanket, a wounded gunner from this battery, the left side of whose head had been struck by a cannon ball, and his brains, in the unbroken membrane (like a bag) hung on his shoulder. I remon-

---

* On the first, or second day of the operation of No. 7 Battery.

strated on the uselessness of dragging this poor expiring man to the camp, the half of his head having been shot away. They laid him down to rest themselves and consider, at which moment he expired, and his jaw dropped; and judging that the men had no objection to be employed out of the battery, I recommended them to bury their comrade on the spot, and return immediately to the battery, where they were much required. Soon after, I met some more artillery-men conveying (also in a blanket) from the same battery, an artillery officer, (Capt. Dundas,) very severely wounded, he was a heavy man, and his left arm dreadfully shattered, the shirt and coat torn to rags, his arm was bent and hung over the side, and the weight of his body swagged to the ground. I stopped to assist in putting him in a better position, and laid his left arm straight by his side—his left thigh and leg were also injured. The men proceded with him to the camp. I then passed on to the battery, as a spectator, it was indeed in ruins, the embrasures and buttresses, and nearly all the parapet, were demolished and open to the town;—it was intensely hot— I remained ten minutes.

The embrasures were repaired, and the bombardment continued vehemently ; — the enemy, also, threw some shot and shells in rapid succession.

I proceeded to my duty at the construction of No. 8 breaching battery, where a shell passed over and near me, and sunk into the soft earth of the glacis: having watched it for some time, and remarked to a man by my side, that I thought it would not explode, (I did not then change my position,) imme- diately it exploded; and, hearing the twirling of a fragment coming toward me, I said to the man, " here comes a piece of that shell, take care !"—and stepping a short pace to my left, the man did the same—which placed him, unfortunately, nearly in my former posi- tion—the fragment passed, and entered deep into the wall of sand-bags near us, when the soldier very calmly said, " that struck me, Sir;" and, lifting up his right arm, shewed that his hand was torn in strings. He said, "what shall I do?" I replied, " set off to your camp, to be sure:" and lamented that I had no one to send with him.

Three days before the final assault of Badajos, when employed in converting No. 12 battery, and laying down platforms for ten (I believe) howitzers to cover the advance, all the spare sand-bags were, by desire of Major Burgoyne, to be placed near No. 1 (dismantled) battery, for the convenience of those repairing (from time to time) the breaching batteries. I accompanied the men to shew where to deposit the bags. Two medical officers in blue surtouts and black feathers were here looking into the Town, and invited by the convenience of a scollop in the edge of the bank, had placed their glasses in it. Such scollops were made by round shot from the enemy, but this scollop, I knew from observation, was made, and frequently

brushed, by shots from a gun fixed, I supposed, in the Castle, for the purpose of
throwing shots into the Engineer-Depôt of
implements. I passed to lay down the
bags a few paces from them, intending to
communicate to them their risk, when Lord
Wellington, with an officer, came from the
breaching batteries, gently walking in the
trenches, where shot and shells were flying,
as tranquilly as if strolling in his own lawn
in England, and on approaching the medical officers, they made their obeisance and
offered their glasses, one of which his Lordship politely received, and also placed in
the same scollop: at that instant the besieged (perhaps seeing cocked hats) fired
the gun, the shot hummed as it passed
over Lord Wellington's head, he smiled,
but made his inspection, and returned the
glass. I paid my respects to his Lordship, " en passant," and beheld with aston-
ishment, two private individuals—evidently
Londoners—who enquired of me the *shortest*
way to the breaching batteries. I con-

sented to escort them, and they walked with me; but prostrating themselves at the report of every gun, remarked that I did not " duck," being, they supposed, accustomed to them. On arriving at the end of a new unfinished cut leading from the second parallel direct to the breaching batteries, and near the Town; and being rather waggishly inclined at their request, I informed them this was the *shortest* way, and took leave. I turned back to view them, and beheld both again crouching on " all-fours," but laughing heartily. These Londoners, I have reason to believe, were from Mr. Baker's Panorama, in Leicester Square. [NOTE.—1813. I went on my crutches to view the Panorama of Badajos, where was painted Lord Wellington and the two medical officers, as above mentioned: the artists had not included themselves nor myself, but substituted (for London spectators) a guard in the trenches presenting arms to the Commander-in-chief. And, in the frontispiece of their descrip-

tive pamphlet, was represented, the wounded
French soldier in Fort Picurina.] Excuse
this digression.

I mentioned in the commencement of these
"Recollections," that I had expressed a desire of being employed on any extraordinary
affair; and therefore received, with great
satisfaction, the charge of erecting scaling-
ladders :* and Major Burgoyne, with a spy-
glass, described the mill-dam over which
to lead the troops, and the mound (a half
sugar-loaf) on the top of which to place
five ladders against the wall to reach the
parapet, and one ten feet longer against
the plane face of the same wall on the
right of the mound.—Six ladders were to
be reared by Lieut. Cattenagh, 92d regiment,
and six ladders by Lieut. ——, R.E., but that
the ladders on the mound were much relied
upon.

With these instructions I was highly gra-

* These were the common sort of ladders, such as
are used by builders ; and were made of castano (chestnut)
trees, in the woods by the men of the staff corps.

tified, and several times went on a rising ground with a glass to contemplate the point " d' entrée." My mind was, in truth, very intent, and anxious for the success of the *task I had solicited.*

The duties in the trenches were conducted by the Hon. Major General Colville, Major General Bowes, and Major General Kempt, under the superintendence of Lieut. General Picton. When General Kempt was on duty in the trenches, his vigilance was proverbial with the soldiers of the working parties,— " work away boys, there's one above sees all!"—The Generals were all indefatigable, each remaining on duty twelve hours in the trenches, and were in great danger. General Picton narrowly escaped destruction by a shell which fell upon a man's head in the trench, near No. 3 battery, and exploding at the moment, scattered the man in fragments to the winds.

All the breaching batteries having been completed, directed their vehement bombardment against the bastions of La Trinidad,

Santa Maria, and ravelin of Saint Roque; and practical breaches were effected, but rendered inaccessible by the enemy's unusual and formidable entrenchments and defences.

Lieut. General Sir Thomas Graham and Lieut. General Sir R. Hill by their movements obliged the enemy to retire towards Cordova, leaving a small body of cavalry and infantry at Zalamaca de la Serena; and Marshal Soult having quitted Cadiz on the 23rd and 24th of March, marched upon Seville with all the troops, (except about four thousand men,) and proceeding from thence he arrived on the 4th of April at Llerina, and patrolled with strong detachments of cavalry and infantry to Usagre, some leagues nearer Badajos. In the interim General Ballasteros, profitting by Marshal Soult's departure, immediately occupied the place he had left, where his army was received by the inhabitants with the most joyful acclamations. And General Graham, in anticipation, being prepared to retrograde gradually, as was General Hill, from Don

Benito and the upper parts of the Guadiana, and to dispose their Divisions in demonstration of resistance to Soult's further advance, completely checked his progress.

The crisis for a grand effort to conquer the Fortress had arrived, and the besiegers were urgent. Several councils were held, and opinions expressed; when General Picton, feeling assured of the inaccessibleness of the breaches—which was afterwards proved correct by the severe losses the 4th and Light Divisions sustained—proposed an escalade of the Castle, and explained his plan, undertaking the performance thereof with his Division; and not meeting with the acquiescence anticipated, he retired to his camp to await the " general orders."

The arrangements in progress were completed, and orders were issued for a general assault at 10 o'clock P. M., assigning to General Picton the escalade of the Castle. The plan was, that Lieut. Gen. Picton should attack the Castle by escalade with the 3rd Division; a detachment from the guard in the trenches

c

of the 4th Division, under the command of Major Wilson, 48th regiment, should attack the ravelin of Saint Roque; the 4th Division, under the Hon. Major General Colville, with the Light Division, under Lieut. Colonel Barnard, to attack the breaches in the bastions of la Trinidad and Santa Maria, and the curtain by which they were connected; the 5th Division, under General Leith, to occupy the ground which the 4th and Light Divisions had occupied during the siege; and Lieut. General Leith to make false attacks upon the outwork Pardileras, and another on the Fort towards the Guadiana, with the left Brigade of the Division under Major-General Walker, which he was to turn into a real attack, if circumstances should prove favorable; Brigadier General Power, with his Portuguese Brigade, to make false attacks on the Tete-du-Pont, the Fort of Saint Christoval, and the new redoubt Mon Cœur. By which it appears that the main attacks were the Castle and the breaches; the latter aided by the attack on the ravelin of St. Roque, and all, by the simultaneous false attacks on various points.

The attack of the Fortress was intended on the night of the 5th of April, and myself and others were ordered to attend General Picton in his tent, at eight o'clock in the evening; but the assault was delayed another day, and a breach (3rd) was effected in the curtain of la Trinidad.

To attempt fully to describe the hilarity of the officers and soldiers, individually preparing for a premeditated attack, would be extremely difficult;—the officers with their servants carefully packing their portmanteaus, and the soldiers in like manner packing their knapsacks, to leave in their encampment secure, so as to be readily found on their return,—without, for one moment, considering the certainty of all not returning; the men fixing their best flints in their muskets, and all forming in column, with the utmost alacrity, to march to the assault, deserve the admiration and lasting gratitude of their country. Alas! of all those ardent fellows, many, many never returned.

On the 6th, all minds were anxious for
the "advance," and orders were issued for
the attack at ten o'clock that night. I again,
with Major Burgoyne, attended by appoint-
ment General Picton, at eight o'clock P. M.:
General Kempt and several others were there.
General Picton having explained his arrangements and given his orders, pulled out his
watch, and said, "It is time, gentlemen, to
go:" and added, emphatically, "Some persons
are of opinion that the attack on the Castle
will not succeed, but I will forfeit my life
if it does not!"

We returned to the Engineer-Depôt, where
the fatigue-party and others had assembled
to receive ladders, axes, &c., which General
Picton superintended himself, and repeated
to them some directions. He then asked,
"Who is to show me the way?" and Major
Burgoyne presented me to him. When the
General had sent off the party, he turned to
me,—"Now, sir, I am going to my Division,"
—and rode away. I followed and soon lost
sight of him in the dark, but pursuing the
same direction, (not knowing where the

Division was,) I fortunately arrived at the Division, which was drawn up in column between two hills, at the distance, I supposed, of three miles, and quite out of sight of Badajos. General Picton having addressed each of the Brigades, he returned to the head of the Division, ordered the "march," and said to me, "Now, sir, which way are we to go?" We proceeded a considerable distance, and again came within sight of the Fortress; the lights of which were altered and much extended.

I was to conduct to a certain point in the trenches to meet Major Burgoyne, and thence to the escalade; and naturally felt the weight of the charge, when afar in strange ground, where none had before trod; for, if I had misconducted, so that *this* Division arrived too late,* I cannot, even now, ruminate on the result. But, I had been so perfectly instructed by Major Burgoyne, that

* Which happened to a distant Division, by the guide mistaking his way.

I could not err; notwithstanding, to prevent
the possibility of deviating, I several times
ran ahead to ascertain the correctness of
my guidance towards the given point; the
General inquiring each time if we were going
right, I confidently answered in the affirma-
tive. Again I departed, and approaching in
the direction of the ravelin, but far from
it, stumbled on a dead soldier of the 52nd
regiment, in a spot where I considered he
must have been killed in repulsing a sortie
of the enemy; which, operating as a land-
mark, proved that I was perfectly correct.
—No delay or error occurred—I returned
to the column, and informed the General that
it was necessary to incline to the right; and,
coming to the side of the Talavera road, the
column descended into it. Here General
Picton, dismounting, sent away his horse,
and HEADED HIS DIVISION ON FOOT.

The firing of the enemy's musketry becoming brisk, increased the General's anxiety to
be as contiguous as possible, previous to the
general assault, lest any occurrence should

retard the operation of his Division : and
when I had again advanced some distance,
to discover Major Burgoyne, and returned,
General Picton, emphatically expressing himself, said that I was blind, he supposed, and
going wrong; and, drawing his sword, swore
he would cut me down. I explained, and
he was appeased. I was fully sensible of
the high responsibility the General felt for
the success of his own proposition of escalading the Castle, (and the more so, as myself
solicited the task *I* had undertaken to per-
form,) which, added to the prompt decision
and intrepidity of character by which General
Picton was so eminently distinguished, ope-
rated strongly on his mind; and in my own
bosom lamented his unnecessary precipitancy,
— but I could not repress an involuntary
admiration of his ardour! and glanced at
the interesting picture of the General, sword-
in-hand, and myself before him assuring him
of my correctness. We soon after arrived
at the very spot, in the first parallel, where
Major Burgoyne was waiting; when, seizing

his hand, with the affection of a brother-
soldier at such a moment, I expressed my
happiness on the perfection of my guidance,
and my assurance to the General that "I
had not led him an inch out of the way."
Indeed it was as correct as a line.

The Division then entered the trench, and
proceeded nearly to the end of it, when the
enemy's volcanic fire burst forth in every
direction long and far over the Division, and
in every kind of combustible. The grandeur
of the scene, as Colonel Jones says, was
indescribable; but some idea may be formed
of its refulgence, by supposing it possible
that all the stars, planets, and meteors of the
firmament, with innumerable moons emitting
smaller ones in their course, were congregated
together, and descending upon the heads of
the besiegers. Such was the appearance of
the fire, raining from the besieged; it was
as light as day.—General Picton exclaimed,—"Some of them are too soon; what
o'clock is it?" and, comparing his watch
with others, the time was *a quarter before*

ten o'clock. I mention this, because it has
been supposed that General Picton's Division
approached too soon. When the Division had
advanced some distance from the parallel,
and General Picton at its head, with General
Kempt, Colonel Burgoyne, the staff, and myself, the enemy's fire increased considerably,
and I was walking between General Picton
and General Kempt, when General Picton
stumbled and dropped wounded in the foot.
He was instantly assisted to the left of the
column; and the command devolving on General Kempt, he continued to lead it with the
greatest gallantry! On arrival at the mill-
dam (extremely narrow), over which the
troops were to pass, streams of fire blazed
on the Division: the party with ladders, axes,
&c., which had preceded, were overwhelmed,
mingled in a dense crowd, and stopped the
way; being by the side of General Kempt,
I said, for recognition sake if we survived,
" This is a glorious night, sir; a glorious
night!" and rushing through the crowd,
(numbers were sliding into the water and

drowning,) I found the ladders left on the palisades in the fosse, and this barrier unbroken; in the exigence, I cried out, "Down with the paling!" and, aided by the officers and men in rocking the fence, made the opening at which the Division entered; and which being opposite the before-mentioned mound, then, " Up with the ladders !"— " What ! up here ?" said a brave officer, (45th). " Yes !" was replied—and all seizing the ladders, pulled and pushed each other with them up the acclivity of the mound, as the shortest way to its summit. The above officer, and a Major of Brigade, laboriously assisted in raising the ladders against the wall, where the fire was so destructive that with difficulty five ladders were reared on the mound, and I arranged the troops on them successively, according to my instructions, during which I was visited by General Kempt and Major Burgoyne, although this place, and the whole face of the wall, being opposed by the guns of the Citadel, were so swept by their discharges of round-shot, broken shells, bundles of cartridges, and other missiles, and also from the top of the wall, ignited shells, &c., that it was almost impossible to twinkle the eye on any man before he was knocked down. In such an extremity, four of my ladders with troops on them, and an officer on the top of each, were broken, successively, near the upper ends, and slided into the angle of the abutment;—dreadful their fall, and appalling their appearance at day-light. I was forced to the most excessive perseverance of human exertion, and cheered to excite emulation, "Huzza! they are long enough, push them up again." On the remaining ladder was no officer; but, a private soldier at the top, in attempting to go over the wall, was shot in the head, as soon as he appeared above the parapet, and tumbled backwards to the ground; when the next man [45th regiment] to him upon the ladder instantly sprang over!!! If he was *not* killed, he certainly DESERVED A CROWN OF GLORY in this world; and, if he *was* killed, and brave soldiers are favored IN HEAVEN, HE THERE, NO DOUBT, RECEIVED HIS REWARD! But, so numerous were the INTREPID, that the man above-mentioned could only be distinguished as ONE of the "BRAVEST OF THE BRAVE." I instantly cheered "Huzza, there is one over, follow him!" but the circumstance of the ladders being broken, delayed the escaladers in this part a short time, until the ladders were replaced, so as to reach *near* the top of the wall, which enabled the troops to pass over; and I frequently cheered, accompanied by the men, to give notice of the successful perseverance of the escaladers to the distant assailants; whose responsive cheers were distinctly heard to be continued around the Fortress.

The 4th and Light Divisions advanced to the assault of the breaches led by their gallant officers, with the utmost intrepidity; but the unusual obstacles prepared by the enemy on the summit, and in rear of the breaches proved so formidable, that our soldiers could not establish themselves; and many brave officers and men, in their perseverance to penetrate, were in succession killed or wounded by explosions on the top of the breaches. The 4th and Light Divisions were, therefore, ordered to retire to the ground they had assembled on immediately preceding the attack:——REMNANTS as they were of those NOBLE DIVISIONS which stood on that ground two short hours before.

The fire of the 4th and Light Divisions, at the breaches, having ceased, enabled the enemy to augment the opposition in these parts, and increase the fire upon the 3rd Division.

About this time General Kempt was wounded: his exertions had been most arduous in bravely visiting, and directing EVERY POINT OF ATTACK, THROUGH THE HEAVIEST FIRE!

After I had arranged the replaced ladders, and in returning to the longest ladder, planted against the wall on the right of the mound, it was my turn to fall—my right thigh was fractured by a ball which entered

the upper part, and I fell on a man who had
just dropped at my side, with the calf of my
leg and heel turned upwards. I instantly
seized the trousers, and turned over the limb
to preserve existence; and being in a spot
most exposed to the guns, I requested a
field-officer* near to desire some of his men
to carry me out of the stream of fire; but
(I had occasion to mention him to General
Kempt on the mound) he turned himself
away,— and one of his men immediately
said, " I'll take you down, sir; can you
stand?"—This good fellow took me on his
back, but was obliged to drop me, and in a
place more exposed. While here, an officer
of the 83rd regiment, without his hat, came
staggering behind me; and, on approaching,
inquired how I was hurt; said he was
wounded in the head, and that he would
stay by me for mutual consolation, and sat
down; but as my spasms were extremely
severe, and regular as the pulse, I had no

---

* This officer, I have reason to believe, was killed at
  Burgos.

interval for conversation; he left me, and placed himself with his back against the palisades, near the opening, on which the enemy's shots continued to rattle. I saw him in the same position at day-break, but knew not if he was alive or dead. Two other men whom I requested to remove me, were also obliged to set me down—unfortunately—at the base of the mound, with my fractured limb placed upwards on the bank, so that I could only support myself by placing my hands behind, to prop me in a sitting position; in which I remained immovable till late in the afternoon of the next day, amongst numerous brother sufferers.

The escaladers persevered amidst the determined opposition of the besieged; and the contest at the castle-wall was desperate, the besieged throwing down broken waggons, beams, shot and shells, on the besiegers, and endeavoured to drag the ladders, from the men below.

Lieut. Mc. Alpin, 88th regiment, supposed to have been the first who mounted the castle-

wall, was there killed.—Several claimed to
have been the first up; but, so ardent were
all to gain the summit and spring over to
the conquest, that it was difficult for the
individuals to decide who the first was, as
the intrepidity of our troops seemed to have
increased in proportion to their difficulties,
and to avenge the fall of their Generals, and
of their numerous comrades who lay strewed
around. It was, indeed, delightful to hear
our buglers upon the wall near the citadel,
sounding the animating " ADVANCE," to pro-
claim their success, and accelerate the distant
troops; which consoled the wounded, and
ameliorated their pangs. One bold bugler
as soon as he mounted the wall,—deter-
mining to be first,—when sounding the " Advance," was killed in the act of blasting
forth his triumphal music.—The Portuguese
Brigade arriving, turned to the right towards
the citadel.

Numbers of heroes fell on both sides;—at
the castle the bodies of the English and
French laid upon each other;—but, General

Picton's Division conquered, and was established before twelve o'clock in the citadel,

"The greater part performed, achieve the less!"

DRYDEN.

which commanded all the works of the Town,
and in the Town; and enabled the other
Divisions—which had been powerfully resisted—to enter the Town.

The first person who entered the Town
was the gallant Lord Fitz-Roy Somerset, then
Secretary to the Commander of the Forces,
who, to ascertain the state of the 3rd Division,
bravely forced his way through the innumerable obstacles, and imminent dangers of the
Town, to the Castle, which he entered, found
the 3rd Division established, and reposing
in security.

The ravelin of St. Roque was also carried,
with the assistance of Major Squires, R. E.,
by Major Wilson's (48th) detachment of two
hundred men, from the guard in the trenches.

Major General Walker advanced with his
Brigade, from the barrier on the Olivença

D

road, to make a false attack, entered the covered-way on the left of the bastion of Saint Vincent, and availing himself of the circumstances of the moment, he with great military skill pushed forward, and gallantly escaladed the *face* of that bastion. Here he was most dangerously wounded.

The 4th and Light Divisions having again formed for the attack, all resistance ceased; and in the morning General Phillipon surrendered, with General Veilande, his staff, and garrison, which he stated consisted of upwards of five thousand men at the commencement, near twelve hundred were killed and wounded, and that about four thousand were prisoners. The garrison, composed of picked men, made a fine appearance when they marched out, after having delivered up their arms. Phillipon had some of the ablest French officers, particularly the Chief-Engineer.

General Phillipon finding the Castle wrested from him, had retired, or rather took refuge, in Fort Saint Christoval, and though van-

quished, and the whole of the "Impregnable
Fortress" was in the Earl of Wellington's
possession, he ostentatiously assumed in the
morning a CONSIDERATION of CAPITULA-
TING, until a positive message was repeated,
requesting him to attend the Earl of Wellington immediately.

Self-approbation is human nature; and is
a predilection all are subject to in various
degrees, according as diffidence, or its opposite quality, retract or maintain; and, as
all the Divisions exerted their utmost pow-
ers to conquer, all (appreciating their own
efforts) naturally considered themselves the
conquerors; and to them, most justly, is
praise due.

Nevertheless, from the foregoing, and in
reference to the dispatch of Lord Wellington,*
it will be seen that the conquest of the
"impregnable Fortress of Badajos," resulted
from the escalade and possession of the
Castle,—according to General Picton's pre-
diction,—"Some are of opinion that the attack

* Page 64.

on the Castle will not succeed, but I will forfeit my life if it does not."

The loss was very considerable; (which General Picton did me the honor of explaining to me in London,* the day before his departure,) would not have happened if his original plan had been wholly executed: and he added many very special circumstances.

† It has been said, "The plan for attacking Badajos was so extremely hazardous, that, though adopted through necessity, from inability to undertake any other, it never was approved of; and Lord Wellington always entertained great doubts of its success."

† Notwithstanding, so strongly impressed was the mind of General Picton, on the possibility of escalading the Castle, that he pledged his life it would succeed: and so it did, to the dismay of General Phillipon; who, not expecting an attack on the Castle, "had arranged, in the hope of relief from Soult,

---

* When at breakfast with him, at his lodgings in Baker Street.

† The paragraphs above and in page 35 accord.

to hold the Castle, Tete-du-pont, and Fort
Christoval, after the breaches should be
forced.*

It has also been asserted that, " Although
General Picton's successful escalade of the
Castle placed the garrison at his mercy, yet,
the Division remaining therein, produced no
other immediate effect, he not having com-
municated it."—General Picton had not, it
is admitted, the means of communication.

The capture of Badajos, which was the last
strong-hold of the enemy on the frontiers of
Portugal, animated the Portuguese and Spaniards with the most felicitous anticipations of
tranquillity and security; many of the wealthy
immediately returned, and engaged in the
purchasing of lands, building and repairing
dwellings, &c. in Badajos, Elvas, Campo-
Major, and in all the Towns I passed through
towards Lisbon.

There are few examples in history, of For-
tresses of the great strength of Ciudads
Rodrigo and Badajos, having been acquired

* Proved by a document found in the Castle.

with such rapidity on the part of the besiegers.

By these enterprises, and the brilliant
capture and destruction of Fort Napoleon,*
Almarez, the enemy felt the " avenging-
sword," and losing all confidence in his own
strength, the fertile province of Estremadura
became secure from further desolation, and
opened, to the allied army and the auxiliary
guerillas, Madrid, the Andalusias, Catalonia,
and, indeed, the whole of Spain; and obliged
the enemy to facilitate the retrograding of
his columns, by manœuvres (always pointing
towards home) on fastnesses he had not
the power to maintain, and from which his
Generals were successively driven.

The encampment was very extensive, some
of the Divisions six miles distant from the
Fortress:—the Ordnance nearest, and about
three miles. Several of the enemy's shot
and shells reached the camp; and it was
asserted that a shell approached head quar-
ters, and exploded.

* By the 1st Brigade of General Hill's Division.

A Captain of the 42nd regiment, (Monro,) who had arrived in the afternoon of the 6th of April, as a spectator, most gallantly joined the escaladers of the Castle, as a VOLUNTEER, and was killed on the top of a ladder.

An officer I knew, had resolved, on entering the town, to proceed instantly to the church tower, and place his sash upon the flag-staff, above the town colors, in token of victory; but he was severely wounded before an entrance was effected. Many of the soldiers declared during the siege, that, as a compensation for their labor with the pick-axe and spade, they would rummage the town; which they performed for nearly three days; loading themselves with the spoils of bedding, curtains, wearing apparel, plate, &c; and returning to their camp, beating French drums, sounding French bugles, singing, cheering, and exulting in the most extravagant gesticulations and clamors. A soldier offered for sale, at my tent, upwards of twenty silver forks, spoons, and solid knife-handles. Many of the Spanish inhabitants were obliged to go into the camp to purchase their *own* clothes of the soldiers.——

I remained where the soldiers were obliged to drop me, at the base of the mound, amidst expiring brother sufferers.* During the night, the moans, prayers, cries, and exclamations of the wounded, fully expressed the degrees of their agonies, in the varieties of acuteness and cadence of tone, from the highest pitch in the treble to the lowest note in bass. Some of the wounded were, undoubtedly, raving mad, violently vociferating dreadful imprecations and denunciations; others singing; and many calling the numbers of their regiments, (as O! 45th.—O! 74th.—O! 77th.) to attract their comrades to their aid. Many of the fallen heroes received additional wounds during the night. One man sat on my left side, rocking to and fro, with his hands across his stomach; in the morning he was dead, stretched on his back, and bleeding out of three wounds in his head, from shots he subsequently received there: his head rested

* Page 49.

heavily on my hand, which I had not the
power to withdraw.

At day-break the wailings of the wounded
had been either silenced by death, or subsided
by the exhaustion of the survivors; and the
thunder of the guns having ceased on the
previous night, was succeeded by a solemnity,
which now was more awful to us than the
raging of the battle.

The dead and wounded were as close as
a regiment laying down to repose;—

> " With gasps and glassy eyes they lay,
> And reeking limbs immovable."

and this part becoming the readiest road
for the soldiers—stepping between us—from
the Town to the Camp, the cravings for
" water!" and " bearers!" were reiterated
by all, to those who approached or passed;
but they were too intent on their own
sports, except an artillery-man, who beholding my languor, kindly administered
his blue-bottle (which he had filled with
brandy in the church) to my mouth; the

sip revived me, but I was apprehensive of
hemorrhage.—This man promised to send
bearers.* Late in the afternoon, an officer
with bearers came to take up a man of
his regiment, who laid at my side, with
eleven shots in him; and as he was ap-
parently expiring, and could not be moved,
I prevailed on the officer to allow his men
to convey me to my tent; but they were
unwilling, and though obliged to carry me,
jostled, and nearly rolled me out of the
bier in going over the mill-dam; they,
however, laid me down on my left side at
the end of the second parallel, leaving the
bier † under me, and joined the sports in
the Town. I found myself in a very re-

---

* I had strictly ordered my servant to seek for me
among the fallen, if I did not return from the attack in
the morning; but he had remained in charge of my baggage, he said;—but I said, that he had remained, in preference, in charge of a large pot of soup and a bag of wine,
for regaling himself and fellow-servant. I dismissed him
as soon as another could be obtained.

† A bier is a piece of sacking to lay the wounded soldier
upon, with a pole on each side, and carried by four persons.

mote situation, and in danger of remaining undiscovered; in despair, I reached one
of the strewed sand-bags, and placing it
under my head resigned myself to my
fate. Some time afterwards four Spaniards
strolled near and examined me, and I requested them to convey me to the camp:
they consulted, and refused; but as they
were walking off, a surgeon (with buff facings)
—most providentially—approached, and seeing me, compelled the fellows to carry me,
giving them in charge to a sergeant who
was passing, and I arrived at my tent,
where surgeon Fitz Patrick, R. A. immediately attended me; then Colonel Robe,
R. A. and Majors Burgoyne and Squires
visited me, the two latter frequently, and
most kindly expressed their approbation of
my conduct. On the third day I was removed to the Town; and dreading to be
placed in the church among upwards of
five hundred on the stone floor, where the
difficulty of supplying all their necessities
and administering tender care, increased the

sufferings of the wounded patients beyond
the means in the power of the surgeons
to avert, and, in many cases exhaustion and
death ensued, which amongst fewer patients
might have been ameliorated, I preferred
a place alone, and was put into a house
pointed out by a surgeon in the street, who
recognised me, and expressed his happiness
at being able to attend me;—but I did
not see him again for three days, when he
dropped in for a gossip, without examining
or touching my limb. In this manner he,
at his leisure, paid me a few visits; and
I remained until the middle of May, when
my professed friend the doctor called, ex-
pressly, as he said, to put me in a proper
position, and to set my limb, which had been
bent in the fractured part, by the awkward
movements, and he desired my servant to
call in three or four natives to assist. While
the man was gone, the doctor stepped home,
" a few doors;" my servant and the men
came, and having waited for the surgeon until they were tired, strolled away—no doctor

returned.—But, several hours afterward, I heard him scraping on a violoncello he had previously told me that he found in the church. He called in, on the fourth day, for a moment to tell me that he expected his promotion by the next gazette.——I never more saw him. He was succeeded by a truly worthy man, staff-surgeon Burnal, who immediately had me placed comfortably with my mattress upon the (brick) floor, and set my limb with an eighteen-tail bandage, &c.; he continued to attend me; and also on General Walker,* and a Lieutenant of the Rifle corps, being three of the worst cases remaining, and which could not be moved when the army departed.

* General Walker's wound was of a most extraordinarily severe nature—a musket shot cut him across his stomach, grazed the main arteries, which continued oozing for many weeks, hourly threatening hemorrhage; and also detached several ribs from the breast-bone. After a long confinement in Badajos, he was conveyed in his pallet, on men's shoulders, to Lisbon, (a journey of several weeks,) when he embarked for England, and miraculously recovered; and rejoined Lord Wellington's army near Pampeluna, and was again severely wounded.

EXTRACT OF A

DISPATCH FROM THE EARL OF WELLINGTON,

(REFERRED TO,)

Dated, Camp before Badajos, April 7th, 1812.

———

" THE 4th and Light Divisions having found
" it impossible to penetrate the obstacles
" which the enemy had formed to impede
" their progress,"—attempts were " repeated
" till after 12 o'clock at night,"—" and,
" finding, that success was not likely to be
" attained; and that General Picton was es-
" tablished in the Castle, I ordered the 4th
" and Light Divisions to retire."

" —— I have had occasion to mention all
" these officers [Hon. Major General Colville,
" Major General Bowes, Major General Kempt,
" and Lieutenant General Picton,] during the
" course of the operations; and they all dis-

" tinguished themselves, and were all wound-
" ed in the assault." The gallantry and
" conduct of Major General Walker, who was
" also wounded, and that of the officers and
" troops under his command, were highly
" conspicuous."

" I am particularly obliged to Lieutenant
" General Picton for the manner in which
" he arranged the attack of the Castle; and
" for that in which he supported the attack,
" and established the troops in that impor-
" tant post."

" Lieut. General Picton has reported to
" me, particularly, the conduct of Lieut. Col-
" onel Williams, 60th regiment; Lieut. Colonel
" Ridge, 5th regiment, killed in the assault
" of the Castle; Lieut. Colonel Forbes, 45th
" regiment; Lieut. Colonel Fitz-Gerald, 60th
" regiment; Lieut. Colonels Trench and Man-
" ners, 74th regiment; Major Carr, 83rd
" regiment; and the Hon. Major Packenham,
" Assistant Adjutant General to 3rd Division."

" He has likewise particularly reported the
" good conduct of Colonel Campbell, 94th

" regiment, commanding the Hon. Major
" General Colville's Brigade during his ab-
" sence, in command of the 4th Division,
" whose conduct I have so frequently had
" occasion to report to your Lordship."

" The officers and men of the corps of
" Engineers and Artillery were equally dis-
" tinguished during the operations of the
" Siege, and at its close.   Lieut. Colonel Flet-
" cher continued to direct the works, (not-
" withstanding he was wounded in the Sortie,
" 19th March,) which were carried on by
" Major Squires, and Major Burgoyne, under
" his directions. The former established the
" detachment under Major Wilson in the
" ravelin of Saint Roque, on the night of
" the Storm; and the latter attended the
" attack of the 3rd Division on the Castle.—
" I have received reports from the General
" Officers commanding Divisions, of the as-
" sistance they received from the officers of
" those departments attached to them, the
" greatest number of whom, and all their
" personal staff, are wounded."

General Picton has been severely and unjustly censured, in several publications, &c. by those whose minds generated disappointment in proportion to the estimation on which their expectations were founded,— for not having, as was alleged, recommended heroic officers under his command at Rodrigo and Badajos; which he has declared, that was a duty he never neglected, and, in many instances, frequently repeated; and therefore having done his utmost, blame did not attach to him—for instance, " Ever since that time (Badajos) I have made repeated applications in favor of my own Aide-de-camp, who was most severely wounded there, without success; although I consider his promotion, in consequence, due to me as much as my daily pay—nor can I account for the omission."—This declaration of his own feelings—made to myself—and expressed in most benign accents, without a breath of allusion to any person, or complaint, must for ever silence any suspicion of General Picton's neglect; and refutes the animadversions so liberally advanced on the memory of a gallant General—slain on the plains of Waterloo!

It is apparent in the dispatch, that General Picton did report particularly the conduct of the officers in command of corps in his Division. And, it is also stated, that the Generals commanding Divisions had likewise commended the officers of those departments attached to them, although their names were not published. But, so numerous were recommendations, that it was, no doubt, difficult to make selections; which, it is presumed, was the cause of the applications in my favor by General Picton, Colonel Fletcher, Colonel Stewart, and others, being obscured in the multitude. However, I was soon afterwards appointed to a vacant company in my regiment, in the usual course. Nevertheless, as honor was my reward—which I am fully sensible of, and highly esteem—I cherish the hope of that honor being illumined by some token, in acknowledgement of my voluntary exertions and sufferings at Badajos: as also in Sir John Moore's retreat, and wound at the Battle of Corunna.

General Picton's friendly letters and kindness to me after his return from the Peninsula, and lastly on the morning previous to his departure for Waterloo, are most gratefully esteemed by me as proofs of his estimation of my conduct, particularly, when he gave me his hand at parting as we walked together from his door, with this assurance, that " I will not quit the Duke of Wellington without convincing him of your services."

This is further evidence of General Picton's attention to the interests of those who had served under his command; and also of the natural amiableness of his noble disposition!

THE DEEDS HE DID, FAME DELIGHTS TO TELL,
AND MOCK OBLIVION'S POWER!—AT WATERLOO HE FELL.

M.

1st July, 1836.

THE

STORMING OF FORT NAPOLEON,

ALMAREZ.

THE Siege of Badajos having terminated by the capture of that powerful Fortress, with all its garrison, stores, &c., the Divisions of the enemy's army retired from Alentejo and Spanish Estremadura; the next object of the Earl of Wellington, was a considerable Fortification forming the grand pass, at Almarez, midway between Badajos and Madrid, eighty English miles from the former, ninety-six miles from the latter, thirty miles from Truxillo, and sixty miles from Merida, situated on the right bank of the Tagus; consisting of Fort Napoleon, strongly fortified, with double ditch, and armed with eighteen twenty-four pounders, and other ordnance; and connected by a floating bridge with a battery of six guns on the opposite side of the river, possessing a numerous garrison well supplied with all kinds of stores, and, being in the general route from the grand arsenal Seville, (via) Badajos, Truxillo, and Toledo, to Madrid, was an obstacle of immediate consideration, the destruction of which was confided to Lieut. General Sir Rowland Hill (now Lord Hill, Commanding-in-chief,) who marched his Division from Almandralejo to Merida and Truxillo, and issued orders for his 1st Brigade to attack Fort Napoleon by storm, on the night of the 18th or before daylight on the 19th of May, 1812.

The 2nd Brigade was directed to make a false attack on the front of a Castle, containing a small garrison, situated on the peak of a mountain (like a sugar-loaf,) which was seated on the one side of the pass it formed on the main road from Truxillo, about four miles from Almarez, and a deep extensive wooded valley on the other side, while the 1st Brigade proceeded circuitously through the valley by the base of the mountain.

The 1st Brigade (50th, 71st, and 92nd regiments) was conducted by experienced guides in the mazy sheep-walks in the brush-wood, which were considered impassable, and arrived near the Fort when the enemy had no suspicion of assailants in that direction. The march was consequently difficult, and so tedious, that the whole of the 50th regiment and the left wing of the 71st Light Infantry, only, were able to thread their way to Fort Napoleon by six o'clock in the morning of the 19th of May, when the sun was shining so resplendent, that as each individual emerged from the labyrinth he was distinguishable, and obliged to lay down (in ambush) to avoid discovery from the battlements; therefore Lieut. Colonel Stewart, (50th regiment) in command of the Brigade, obtained permission to attack Fort Napoleon with this portion only, in preference to the lapse of several hours

in waiting the arrival of the remainder of
the Brigade,—and knowing that his men
would be discovered as soon as they stood
up, the batteries open upon them, and
numbers destroyed while instinctively discharging their firelocks at the enemy on
the ramparts, he judiciously considered that
the only plan was by a simultaneous rush
to the wall, where the cannon had less
effect, and then, instantly to escalade. He
therefore gave strict orders that no man
should load his musket until his arrival
under the walls, and strongly recommended
the use of the bayonet. Colonel Stewart
had described in his regimental orders, previously, the use of the bayonet, and directed
that time should not be wasted in the over
application of the bayonet on any one individual—a touch of a few inches being
sufficient:—meaning, that equal justice should
be administered to all opposers, by the
compliment—" en passant "—of the British
bayonet only.

Our soldiers were formed for the assault
in three Divisions, and advanced, preceded

by the men bearing ladders, through the
enemy's tremendous fire, which instantly
showered upon them, sweeping away all the
men carrying one ladder, but which was
caught up and conveyed by others. Notwithstanding, all the ladders were immediately planted against the walls, but being
rather short, exposed the escaladers to the
rapid fire of the enemy's musketry within,
while in the act of scrambling over the
parapet; and Captain Candler (50th regiment) resolving to lead his company (as
did all the officers) went first up his ladder, was pierced by several balls on the
top of the wall and dropped dead inside.
The escalade was not confined to the ladders only: our soldiers were impatient, and
climbing dilapidated parts, pulled up their
comrades, laid in the inner ditch till all
were gathered, and then dashed forward—
Colonel Stewart himself gallantly leading.

The assault was impetuous, and though
the enemy continued to discharge from the
twenty-four pounders grape and round shot,
and showers from musketry, our fellows

scampered up the ladders and over the ramparts in defiance of the *desperate resistance;*
which so astonished the enemy that the
garrison fled out of the Fort to the bridge,
in order to gain the opposite battery, pur-
sued by the British; but many of the
French who succeeded in passing over, re-
collecting—" self-preservation to be nature's
law,"—severed their end of the bridge to
secure themselves, which prevented even
the chance of their own comrades' escape;
these were forced again into the Fort by
our soldiers with the bayonet, and numbers
of gallant defenders were slaughtered, es-
pecially in the gateway, where the conflict
was severe. Those of the enemy who had
escaped over and broke the bridge, flew
in desperation to the opposite battery and
fired indiscriminately into the Fort, the guns
of which were turned on that battery, which,
with its magazine, was entirely destroyed,
with most of its defenders.

Thus, was Fort Napoleon possessed with
all its ordnance, stores, &c., and the garrison made prisoners, within half an hour.

The Governor finding his strongly armed Fortress, with a garrison of three thousand men, surprised and conquered so instantaneously by a British regiment and a half—about twelve hundred men—became frantic, refusing to surrender his sword, and flourishing it in defiance attempted to strike an officer of the 50th, who was remonstrating with him, when a sergeant, in the warmth of the moment, unfortunately wounded him with his pike, which was deplored as unnecessary; because the poor man with his whole garrison being absolutely prisoners of war, his excitement must soon have subsided. Every assistance and consolation were administered to him; but he, as also others of the wounded on both sides, after eight days' journey to Merida expired there.

In the Fort was a French artillery officer's wife; she was dressed in a kind of male attire, (as a personal security it was supposed,) but which was her equestrian costume, a travelling cap, pelisse, and Turkish trowsers, adapted for her mode of riding on horseback, (like a man,) to whom

the British officers instantly gave protection;
but, the soldiers in the first moments of
victory having rummaged the apartments,
she lost all her baggage and considerable
property before the officers were aware of
it; however, some of her wardrobe and
other articles were collected and restored
to her, but every endeavour to recover
for her from the despoilers (amongst whom
were some French soldiers) the whole of her
property, was unsuccessful, although rewards
were offered—and she quitted the Fort in
grief, leaning on the arms of her husband
and Captain Stapleton, 50th regiment. She
was afterwards accommodated with a horse,
and rode the remainder of the journey, accompanied by her husband.

The prisoners were sent off under the usual
escort; and the conquerors bivouacked on the
heights they had descended from in the
morning, during the removal of the wounded
—burying the dead—arranging transportable
stores—and the demolition of the fortifica-
tions.

While the assault on Fort Napoleon was

proceeding, the remainder of General Hill's Division possessed all the neighbourhood.

The right wing of the 71st Light Infantry, and the 92nd regiment (Highlanders,) were detached to carry the entrenched houses at the bridge, and cut off the enemy's retreat; by proceeding circuitously they arrived, burned the bridge, destroyed the temporary barracks, and joined in the general devastation, the blowing up of the magazine, and the *entire destruction* of Fort Napoleon, and the whole Grand Pass of Almarez: which being completed, the Division returned to Merida, (via) Truxillo, leaving the small Castle with its few soldiers destitute on the mountain, and considered by the General not worth further trouble. The poor devils remained as long as they could subsist, and crept off towards their army, without the probability of ever reaching it.

General Sir Rowland Hill embraced the earliest opportunity of expressing himself to all the officers, personally, and to the men, generally, in terms of the highest approbation of their conduct; which was repeated in general orders.

The loss of the 50th regiment in the assault of Fort Napoleon, 19th May, 1812.—

KILLED.

1 Captain—Candler.—26 Rank and file.

WOUNDED.

1 Captain—Sandys, severely, since dead,

3 Lieuts.—Richardson, severely,

—— John Patterson, slightly,

—— Hemsworth, severely,

3 Ensigns—Godfrey, slightly,

—— Crofton, slightly,

—— Goddard, severely,

1 Sergeant Major—5 Sergeants—87 Rank and file.

Total 50th Regt. killed and wounded 126.

The loss of the left wing of 71st regiment was 1 Captain, severely wounded; and of other officers and rank and file, in proportion to the 50th;—the Captain survived only a few hours.

THE

BATTLE OF CORUNNA.

Sir John Moore's Army was intended
(with the organization and co-operation of
the national corps) to preserve Spain from
the power of the French, and re-establish
its tranquillity; but to such excess were
the political jealousies, and intrigues of trai-
tors to their own nation, that the schemes in
progress for the absolute sale and delivery
of Sir John Moore's Army, by the Spanish
Patriots, into the hands of the French Inva-
ders, were near completion, when General
Moore's indefatigable penetration discovered
that the pretended difficulties of the Juntas,
their apprehensions, irresolutions, delays, and
at last their total apathy, were designs,
only to allure him. He, therefore, finding
the Spanish Corps disbanded, and himself

unsupported, determined on withdrawing his
army towards his ships, and, from Spain,
should the latter become his only alternative;
and he commenced his retrograde in an acute
angle, when on the march to Valladolid, and
turned towards Corunna; this was instinctively
discerned by the soldiers, sagaciously remark-
ing after a night-march, that, " the sun,
yesterday morning, rose on our right-side;
and this morning, it rises nearly on our left;
—we must have made a sharp turn."

Abandoned and deceived by our Spanish
friends—to the utmost of their abilities—it
became necessary for Sir John Moore to return to his ships. His masterly retreat in
the midst of an inclement winter,—pressed by
the overwhelming legions of Napoleon, and
through unusual impediments of dilapidated
towns, snow-covered mountains, craggy pre-
cipices, and deep rivers, the troops enduring
severe fatigue and privations,—terminated by
the glorious battle of Corunna.

On entering Corunna, 11th January, 1809,
the narrator's regiment was quartered in a

convent in the Citadel, where he was snugly
lodged in a closet, and reposed comfortably
upon a shelf, kindly permitting a friend to
lay on another below him; and shutting the
door, they were secure from intruders; with
the luxury of putting off shoes only, (hourly
expecting to " fall in,") they soon forgot
their late toils, in sound sleep.

The vessels which had been sent to Vigo
were returning by express, when the enemy,
having brought up his massive columns, formed his line in hostile array in a strong position on the high land which sloped to the
village of Elvina, about two leagues from
Corunna; menacing our defensive lines, post-
ed in front to check his further advance;
but the enemy continuing to display prepara-
tions for attack, General Moore presented his
whole force in opposition, (all the troops having been previously marched out of Corunna,)
and bivouacked in line on the high ground
facing the enemy, having the village of Elvina
in the valley, in front of the right of the
British line, and nearly midway between the

armies. The land, from the left of the enemy's line to the bottom of the declivity, was an inclined plane; and, from the right of the British line, the declivity was in steps of land, or flat fields successively below each other. On an angle of the lowest step stood the church, overlooking the village, the road to which wound round the base of the church, down the steep, and through the village to the extreme left of the enemy's line, from which returned a deep lane, skirting the village, and passing within a few yards of the church to the upland on the right of the British line. Between the church and the lane was the priest's house, from which was a path to the lane, through a gap in the bank. Beyond the village, on the right of the British line, but nearer to the enemy's left, was a house with a plantation, in which a picquet of Lord Bentinck's Brigade was placed.

On the morning of the 16th of January, 1809, the enemy having received considerable reinforcements, extended his line very con-

siderably: and we were surprised by seeing
a woman with a baby coming direct from
the enemy's line to us. She was an Irish-
woman, the wife of a soldier of the light
company of the 50th regiment, had lain-in
on the march, was kindly attended by
doctors of the French army, supported at
the expense of Marshal Soult, arrived
with his baggage, and was this morning sent
over with Soult's compliments, that he should
soon visit the 50th regiment. Soon after
the arrival of this woman, our picquet was
drove in, and a battery planted by the enemy
at the house it had occupied. A couple of
shots from a nine-pounder in our encampment
were sent through the house, and made the
fellows scamper out of it; and, as it was
not considered necessary to discharge the gun
again, the enemy expeditiously completed the
battery and opened its fire, under cover of
which the columns advanced in " double
quick" from their left to our right.

Lord William Bentinck's Brigade, 4th—
50th—42nd regiments, being the right of the

British line, was ordered to " fall in." The ensigns of the 50th regiment—Moore and Stewart—unfurled the colours by order of Major Napier; who, in allusion to Marshal Soult's message, bravely (enthusiastically) said, " Open the colours that they may see the 50th!"—himself continuing in front, and the men remaining, sometime, with " ordered arms," loaded, as were the 4th and 42nd, as tranquilly as in a barrack-yard, viewing the enemy and waiting the attack. Several shots from the enemy's battery approached, and one entered the earth at the very toes of the right-centre company—to which the men involuntarily, but respectfully, formed a semi-circle, the captain immediately gave the word " dress!" and the men dressed up on the twirling shot. At this instant the enemy's Light Infantry approached very briskly (beaucoup de courage) within a few paces, firing, and wounded some men of the 50th as they stood like a wall in front of their encampment; but the whole Brigade then receiving the word " forward," advanced, firing and

charging with the bayonet; few of the enemy's foremost escaped the punishment due
to their temerity.

The 4th, or King's regiment, halted at the
first step of land where an open front enabled
them to mow the ranks of the attacking
columns, with a steadiness and certainty that
prevented the enemy's grand object of turning the right, and assured him that his design
was impracticable—but the loss of the 4th
regiment was very considerable.

The 42nd Highland regiment most judiciously took its position on the left of the
village, so that the enemy's columns descending from the line, were not only exposed to
the cross-fire of the 42nd and 4th regiments,
but suffered very severely from the frequent
charges with the bayonets of the brave
Highlanders.

The 50th regiment had no other alternative than to pursue the Light Troops, and
meet the enemy's columns in the village,
which became the place of contention, and
a most severe struggle ensued — the killed

and wounded of the British and French soldiers fell upon each other—so personal was
the contest. Here Major Stanhope was killed,
and the ensigns Moore and Stewart mortally
wounded, as was Lieut. Wilson, in advancing;
he had been in extraordinary high spirits all
the morning, and dressed himself in a new
suit of regimentals, (preserved in the retreat,)
" to meet Master Soult," as he expressed
himself. Major Napier was missing, and
supposed killed, some of the soldiers asserting
that they saw him fall.—He was severely
wounded and made prisoner;—he recovered
and returned to England, in exchange.

When the 50th regiment rushed down from
their camp, in pursuit, an officer seeing the
church on an eminence over the turn of the
road, as has been described, and supposing
it to contain a body of the enemy in ambush;
and beholding, also, the French rapidly fill-
ing the lane so contiguous, he considered it
necessary to oppose them, and prevent the
probability of their turning their fire on the
rear of the 50th regiment, when the latter

had passed. He, therefore, extending his
arms, stopped several of his men, and having
arranged them at the corner of the church,
himself entered the church, which, however,
was empty; but the priest's house, between
the church and the lane, was full of
French soldiers, from the lane. The officer
came out, ran round and rejoined his
men who, being screened by the angle of
the church, kept up a brisk fire upon the
enemy in the lane, and several times cleared
the gap, where a French officer, rather below
the middle stature, with stick in hand, exerted himself most gallantly to supply the
gap; on which his men laid their firelocks,
and killed two and wounded three of this
little band; but fortunately the British officer had picked up a dragoon carabine on
the road near Corunna, which he retained
as a "Friend in need." This he had previously loaded with two small buttons from
the collar of his regimental coat, and having been supplied with French cartridges
at the church, he was enabled to assist his

men by discharging his carabine many times
in defence of his post; and the French
officer at the gap seeming resolved to force
his way at the head of his men, the dragoon carabine rested against the corner of
the church ensured an aim which *for ever
checked his progress,* and his men drew back.
" The defenders of the church" with their officer immediately made a dash at the priest's
house, and the enemy—upwards of twenty—
within it, rushed out, but not being able
to reach the gap, turned suddenly round,
and instead of cutting off the church party,
fled into the house, slapped the door, and
fired at random out of the windows, which
afforded the church party an opportunity
of retiring from their hazardous attempt.

About this time General Moore was mortally wounded on a rising ground behind
the right flank of the 42nd regiment, overlooking the village and the enemy's columns,
and upon an elevation equal to the French
battery. His absence from that spot was
noticed, but it was not then known that he
had fallen.

There is no doubt but the French supposed that a very considerable party of the
50th was in ambush behind the church;
and, therefore, unable to penetrate at that
point, pushed up the lane to assist in gaining the right of the 4th regiment, but there
they were warmly repulsed, and outflanked
by the brave rifle corps, from whom they
suffered severely.

Sixty rounds of fresh ammunition, and an
extra bundle of ten (the latter the men put
into their pockets) were previously issued
to the Brigade, but the 50th regiment having
expended all their ammunition and what
they had collected from their fallen comrades
and the enemy, and being too far advanced
to receive a supply, was obliged to retire
on the step of land above the church, facing
outwards and parallel to the lane. Here
they became a barrier—sustaining the enemy's fire — and making arrangements for
maintaining their position with the bayonet,
kept the enemy at bay—without being possessed of a single cartridge—although nearly
all the left wing of the regiment was exposed

to the enemy, and occasioned the adoption
of the "kneeling position" firelocks in hand,
for some time; but, as many of the men
(towards the left) were shot in the head and
fell dead, the soldiers were obliged to pros-
trate themselves with their muskets in their
grasp—anxiously waiting the return of mes-
sengers for ammunition. This situation the
regiment maintained some time, (and growing
dusk,) when the "Guards" advanced, but
mistaking the orders, halted on the step of
land above, and called to the 50th regiment
that they were come to support them, when
several distant voices exclaimed "no, relieve
the 50th." The Rifles were sharply engaged
at this time in the front. The Guards instantly advanced deploying on their right,
to take up the same ground ; but the officer
leading—if he survives—will remember approaching a wounded officer and another who
sat by him, and was requested by them to
file considerably to his right, or more than
half of his regiment would be thrown into
the enemy's fire, before their line could be
formed.

The loss of the 42nd and 50th regiments were nearly equal, and very severe. Several men of the 50th, who volunteered from the French 70th regiment at Vimeira, were here killed in the ranks of the 50th regiment. Major Campbell 42nd regiment, died of fatigue on his arrival at Plymouth.

The 50th regiment retired to their former camp-ground, where Captain Armstrong had borne the corpse of Major Stanhope and laid him at his great length; he was very tall and slim, (resembling in person his relation Mr. Pitt,) and much esteemed and lamented. He was there interred. Ammunition arrived, and the men prepared to rejoin the combat, but the enemy having been completely repelled on the right, next aimed at the centre, and there likewise repulsed, made a third assault on the left, which was continued to a village on the high road, and like Elvina, became the scene of another desperate struggle, which was gallantly sustained by the 14th Regiment, and the enemy completely vanquished.

Night veiled the combatants, and the

enemy withdrew.leaving the British line considerably advanced: meditating, no doubt, to retrieve the last defeat of his columns by a more powerful assault supported by reinforcements.

During the night of the 16th of January, the embarkation of the remains of the army of the lamented Sir John Moore commenced, except the Brigades of Generals Hill and Beresford, which continued on the Heights; and these were embarked on the 17th, as were all that could be collected as long as the boats could be used; but numbers of men, women, and children, lined the shore opposite the Castle when the fleet departed, amongst whom was a Grenadier officer of the 81st regiment severely wounded, laid by his men upon the shingle, to seek their own safety.

The officer (of the carabine) having been wounded in the left thigh by a man who fired at him twice in the same direction, was more fortunate; he had been conveyed in a waggon, with others, to a convent in the Citadel, and in the morning crawled down to the beach, where he was immediately surrounded by many men of his regiment, amongst whom was his own servant. The greetings of master and man were naturally interesting—" How are you?" and, " How are you, Sir?" The servant had two shots in his shoulder, and arm shattered. All were now dependent on their own exertions, and the officer, after several attempts, having thrown himself upon the edge of the *last* boat, (a last effort,) was dragged in by the collar, and with others placed safely on board a ship.

The enemy finding the British embarked, advanced, established a battery to command the harbour, and opened its fire, as the ships were getting under-weigh, on those which had not cleared out, and upon a particular transport, which had hitched on a point of rock; but the heavy guns of our men-of-war kept the battery in check, and the men from the damaged transport were removed to another.

A fair wind springing up, the whole of the British fleet quitted the harbour, but with longing, lingering looks, for those left behind on the road unable to reach Corunna

—on the field of battle—the gallant Chief in his tomb—and those on the shore, whose hearts palpitating at our departure, sunk in their bosoms as the fleet sunk in the distance from their view.

The loss of the 50th regiment in the battle of Corunna, of the rank and file, could not be accurately ascertained, but the following is the list of officers :—

KILLED.

Major Stanhope—Lieut. Wilson,

Ensign Moore,

Ensign Stewart, } Bearing the Colours.

WOUNDED.

Major Napier, severely,—prisoner,

Captain Clunes, slightly,

Captain Armstrong, slightly,

Lieut. Macdonald, slightly,

Lieut. Mac Carthy, severely.

FINIS.

APPENDIX.

—»»●●●««—

BADAJOS.

NOTE p. 49. Thomas Martin, Esq. of Ballinaherd Castle, M. P., most nobly and gallantly served as a volunteer at the Siege of Badajos, having declined a commission offered him by Lord Berresford. In a letter to the author, Mr. Martin says, " I was a volunteer with the storming party of the 88th regiment, on the night the Castle was taken by the 3rd Division, and was wounded as I was about to mount a ladder; and I shall ever consider that having served as a volunteer on that memorable night, has been the proudest action of my life."

NOTE p. 51. The attack and possession of the Castle, preceded that of the Town, " and enabled the other Divisions, which had been

G

powerfully resisted, to enter the Town;" and in consequence of the ladders of the 5th Division not arriving at the time appointed, (p. 39,) the assault by General Walker's Brigade was later than intended, and considerable loss sustained.

General Walker having found it advantageous, made a *real attack*, and himself leading with extraordinary gallantry,—which could not be exceeded,—his Brigade descended into the ditch, and as stated, (p. 52), escaladed the face of the bastion of St. Vincent, and gained the ramparts, although the ladders (conducted by a party under Major Faunce, 4th regiment) being too short, did not reach the top of the wall, and the men were obliged to push and pull each other up; but an embrasure, without a gun was discovered in the curtain of the wall, by which many officers and men entered. Lieut. Stavely, 4th regiment, was killed on the top of a ladder, and numerous brave assailants fell.

The Brigade was ordered to man the ramparts, and the struggle was severe; when as General Walker was bravely leading his Brigade towards the interior of the breaches, to drive the enemy from thence, he received a most dangerous wound (p. 63) from a ball which struck him on the right side, breaking several ribs and driving in a part of the watch he carried in a small pocket in the breast of his coat. The Brigade continued its progress along the rampart, and the General was alone on the ground. Sometime after, a French soldier came to the spot, to whom General Walker said, " I am an English General Officer, badly wounded, and if you will stay by me until you can find assistance to remove me into a house, I will reward you." The soldier replied, " Si vous êtes Général, vous avez des epaulettes, et de l'argent aussi sans doute."—He then tore off the General's epaulettes, rifled his pockets, and left him. Afterwards, another French soldier approached, to him the General said, " I have just been plundered by one of your comrades, and therefore have nothing to offer you now; but if you will stay by me till some one will assist you to carry me to a house, I will reward you. The man looked sternly at the General in his agony, without replying, and began to load

his musket, the contents of which the General
had no doubt, were intended for him; but when
he had loaded, he said that he would remain
with him; and soon after an English soldier
came, and the two, the English and French
soldier, carried the General to the French hos-
pital, whence he was removed to a private
house.

ALMAREZ.

NOTE p. 77.   The elegant military cap of the
French Commandant of Fort Napoleon, Almarez,
was constantly worn, afterwards, as a trophy by
the drum-major of the 50th regiment.

CORUNNA.

NOTE p. 89.   It is probable, that Lord William Bentinck, commanding the Brigade, saw
from the position he was in, the exertions of the
officer with the carabine and his party at the
corner of the church, (which may recur to his
Lordship's memory,) when the enemy

      " Like waves that follow o'er the sea,
      " Came thickly thundering on."

RETURN OF KILLED AND WOUNDED

Of the Army under the command of His Excellency General The
Earl of Wellington, at the storming of Badajos, 6 to 7 April, 1812.

KILLED.

Artil. Captain Latham—8 rank and file

Eng. Lieuts. Lacelles—De Salubury

Bn. Rgt.

1— 4 Captain Bellingham—lieut. Stavely—2 serj.—28 rank and file

2— 5 Major Ridge—1 serj.—10 rank and file

1—7 Major Singer—capt. Cholwick—lieuts. Ray, Fowler, Pike—2 serj.—42 rank and file

1—23 Capt. Maw—lieut. Collins 3 serj.—19 rank & file

3—27 Capt. Jones—lieuts. Levinge, Simcoe, Whyte,—3 serj.—35 rank and file

28 Capt. Johnson, A.D.C. to Major-Gen. Bowes

2—38 Ensign Evans—1 serj.—11 rank and file

1—40 Lieuts. Greenshields, Ayling—volun. O'Brien—5 serj.—46 rank and file

42 Capt. Munro

1—43 Lieut.-Col. McLeod—lieuts. Harvest, Taggart. 3 serj.—71 rank & file

2—44 Lieuts. Unthank, Argent—2 serj.—35 rank and file

1—45 Capt. Herrick — ensigns McDonnell, Collins—1 serj.—18 rank & file

KILLED.

Bn. Rgt.

1—48 Capt. Brooke—lieut. Chiliot—ensign Barker—3 serj.—29 rank & file

1—52 Capts. Jones, Madden, Poole — lieuts. Booth, Royle — 3 serj. — 50 rank and file

5—60 Lieut. Sterne—4 rank & file

2—83 Capt. Fry—1 serj.—22 rank and file

1—88 Capt. Lindsey — lieuts. Mansfield, McAlpin—4 serj.—25 rank & file

94 Ens. Long—12 rank and file

1—95 ︸ Maj. O'Hare—Capt. Diggle—lieut. Stokes—3 serjeants—24 rank and file

Rifles ︸

3—95 Lieuts. Hovenden, Cary, Allex, Crondace — 9 rank and file

Brunk. 7 rank and file

Portuguese.

3d line Lieut. de Silviera

11 — Lieut.-Col. McDonnell,—(91st British)

23 — Ensign de Cavallo

1stCac. Lieut. St. Valez

3 — Capt. Morphew (R.W.I.R. British)

8 — Capt. Bruning (Y.L.I. British)—Lieut. Pinta de Lousac

Rgt.

77   Lieut.-Gen. Sir Thomas Picton, slightly—Major Gen. Hon. C. Colville, severely

81   Maj. Gen. Kempt, slightly

50   Maj. Gen. Walker, dangerously

6   Maj. Gen. Bowes, severely

7 W.I.   Major Hon. H. Pakenham, asst. adj. gen., severely —Majors Brooke, Perm, asst. q. m. gen., severely

81   Capt. James, D. asst. adj. gen., severely

92   Brig. major McPherson, severely

28   Brig. maj. (capt.) Potter, severely

45   Brig. maj. (capt.) Campbell slightly

30   Brig. maj. (capt.) Machell, severely

71   Captain Spottiswoode, A. D. C. to major-gen. Colville. severely

5   Capt. Bennet, A. D. C. to gen. Kempt, severely

50   Lieut. Johnstone, A. D. C. to gen. Walker, slightly

Hus. 18   Lieut. Harris, A. D. C. to gen. Stewart, slightly

Rl. Art.   12 rank and file

R. Eng.   Capts. Nicholas, Williams —lieut. Emmett, severely—5 rank and file

K.G.A.   Lieut. Gochen, severely

1 Royal   Lieuts. Rae, McNail, acting Engineers, slightly

1— 4   Major Faunce, slightly— capts. Williamson, Wilson, Burke, Hanwell, severely—lieuts. Salvin,

Convey, Boyd, slightly, Dean, Brown, Sheppard, Craster, Aley, severely —ens. Rawlins, Arnold, severely —8 serj.—1 d. 164 rank & file

2— 5   Capt. Doyle—lieut. J. Pennington—ens. Hopkins, severely—3 serj.—1 d. 26 rank and file

1— 7   Lieut.-colonel Blakeney— capt. Mair—lieuts. St. Pol, Moses, Devey, Barrington, Lester, Russell, George, severely; Henry, Baldwin, Knowles, slightly—11 serj.—108 rank and file

1—23   Capts. Leckey, Stainforth, sevrly.; Hawtyn, sltly. —lieuts. Johnson, Harrison, Tucker, G. Brown, Farmer, Walker, Brownson, Fielding, Whaley, Holmes, Winyates, Llewelyn, severely—7 serj. —1 d.—84 rank & file —1 serj. and 19 rank & file missing

3—27   Major Erskine (L.C.) severely — captain Ward (L. C.) ditto — lieuts. Thompson, Ratcliffe, severely; Gordon, Moore, Hanbey, Pollock, Weir, slightly—adj. Davidson, severely — ens. Warrington, ditto, died—9 serj.—123 rank & file

2—30   Major Grey (L.C.) sevrly died — capts. Hitchin, slightly: Chambers, severely — lieuts. Baillie,

Bn. Rgt.

Neville, slightly—ens.
Pratt, slightly—6 serj.
—82 rank and file

2—38 Capt. Barnard, severely—
lieuts. Magill, Lawrence,
severely — ens. Reed,
severely—1 serj.—1 d.
28 rank and file

1—40 Lieut.-colonel Harcourt—
maj. Gillies — captains
Phillips, sevrly; Bowen,
slightly—lieuts. Street,
Grey, Moore, Turton,
Butler, Millar, Anthony,
Toole, severely; Gor-
man, slightly — ensign
Johnson, sevrly. volun-
teer Widenham, ditto—
11 serj.—162 rank & file

1—43 Major Wells, severely—
capts. Ferguson, Stroud,
slightly—lieuts. Pollock
Rideout, Capell, W.
Freer, (right arm am-
putated) Oglander (left
arm amputated), Mad-
den, E. Freer, Consa-
dine, Bailie, severely;
Hodgson, O'Connell,
Cook, slightly—16 serj.
1 d.—238 rank & file

2—44 Lieut.-col. H. G. Carlton,
severely — capts. Ber-
wick, Brugh, Jervoise,
severely—lieuts. Mead,
slightly; Sinclair, se-
verely — ens. O'Reilly,
slightly—1 serj.—1 d.
—80 rank and file

1—45 Capts. Lightfoot, Flaharty,
slightly—lieuts. Powell,
Reynett, Metcalfe, se-
verely; McPherson,

Bn. Rgt

Dale, Monroe, slightly
—ens. Stewart, slightly
Jones, severely — vol.
Percy, ditto—8 serj.—
1 d.—55 rank & file

1—48 Lieut.-col. Erskine, severely—major Wilson,
ditto—capts. Bell, Turn-
penny, slightly; French,
severely—lieuts. Brook,
severely; Stroud, Cuth-
bertson, Robinson, Arm-
strong, Wilson, Pount-
ney, slightly—ensigns
Thatcher, Johnson,
Bourke, Thompson, slt.
—6 serj.—116 rank &
file

1—50 Lieut. MacCarthy, asst.-
engineer, severely

1—52 Lieut.-col. Gibbs, severely
—maj. Mein, ditto—
captains R. Campbell,
ditto, Merry, ditto, died
—lieuts. McNair, Kin-
lock, York, Davis, Royds,
slightly; Blackwood,
Barlow, C. Dawson,
severely—ens. Gawler,
slightly—adj. Winter-
bottom, ditto—18 serj.
234 rank and file

5—60 Lieut.-cols. Williams, Fitz-
gerald, slightly —lieut.
Gilse, ditto—adj. Bro-
ety, leg amptd., died—
2 serj.—24 rank & file

74 Lieut.-col. Hon. P. French
severely—capts. Lang-
lands, severely; Thomp-
son, slightly — lieuts.
Grant, King, severely;
Pattison, Ironside, slty.

Bn. Rgt.

—3 serj.—30 rank and file—2 rank and file missing

77 Lieut.-col.Duncan,sltly.— lieuts. Clarke, severely; Pennefather, slightly— adj. Jones, slightly— 2 serg.—8 rank & file

2—83 Lieuts. Bowles, O'Neil, Bloomfield, severely; Barry, FitzGibbon, slt.; ens. Vavasour, Lane, ditto—vol. Illera, ditto. 3 serj.—36 rank & file

1—88 Capts. Murphy, (m.) sev. Peshall, sltly.—lieuts. Davern,sltly.Cockburn, Whitelaw,sev. Stewart, sev.died—ens.Grattan, sevrly.—9 serg.—1 d. 96 rank and file

92 Lieut. Cattenaugh, acting eng., slightly

94 Lieut. Bogue, severely— 6 serj.—46 rank & file

1—95 Captains Crampton, Bal-
      vaired, Grey, McDer-
      mid, slightly — lieuts.
      Johnson, Gardiner,
Rifles. Manners, McPherson,
      Forster, severely; Fitz-
      maurice, slightly — 15
      serj.—3 d. — 136 rank
      and file

3—95 Lieuts. McDonald, Wors-
      ley, Stewart, severely;
      Farmer, slightly—vol.
      Lawson, ditto—2 serj.
      45 rank and file

Brunsk. Capt. Girswald, severely
      —lieut.Kunowskey,slt.

Portug. Br.-gen. Harvey (79Brit.)
      severely—capt.Peacock

Bn. Rgt.

(44 Brit.) brig.-major, severely—lieut. Alvaro di Costa, A. D. C. to gen. Harvey, severely —majs. Tullock, (Brit. artil.,) Anderson, (42 Brit.,) severely—capts. J. de Mattos, severely ; F. de Almeida, J.Maria, slightly — lieuts. de la Serda, ditto; Clements, Pinto, dos Santos Ceb-ral, severely—ens. Go-noon, Tavary, Oliva, d'Alverida, severely; Gos. Bernido, slightly

15 Capt. T. O'Neil (32 Brit.) severely —ens. Poulal, severely

21 Lieut Peruva, severely

23 Capt. R. Felix, slightly— lieuts. Rebocho, Madie-ras, ditto—ens. Men-dorca, slightly ; Pedro Retocho, Servieca, sev.

Caca. 1 Maj. Algeo (34 British) severely—captain Mac Donald, (71 Brit.) ditto ens. Rebello, ditto

3 Lieut.-col. Elder, (95 Br.) —major de Selviera— capts. Ignacio, Dobbin, (27 Br.)—lieuts.Paxato D'Ainderido—ens.Fex-eira, severely

6 Captain O'Hara (47 Br.) slightly — lieuts. Ca-mancho, sev ; Graves, slightly—ens. Jose de Almeida, ditto

8 Capt. Magelaens, sev.— lieut. Condose, slightly ens. Lecha, ditto

POSTSCRIPT.

Copy of General Sir Thomas Picton's reply to the *private* letter alluded to in the "Address."

" Glamorganshire, 4th Nov., 1812.

" My Dear Sir,

" Your letter of the 27th ult. reached me in this Country.

" I shall be in London early in December, when I shall have great satisfaction in giving your claims every support in my power.

" Your very faithful

humble Servant,

THOS. PICTON.

" Lieut. Mac Carthy,
50th Regt."

Franked,   " Cardiff, Nov. 6th, 1812.

Lieut. Mac Carthy,

50th Regt.

" Free,   Lewes,

Thos. Wyndham."   Sussex."

Also published in facsimile in *The Spellmount Library of Military History* and available from all good bookshops. In case of difficulty, please contact Spellmount Publishers (01580 893730).

HAMILTON'S CAMPAIGN WITH MOORE AND WELLINGTON DURING THE PENINSULAR WAR by Sergeant Anthony Hamilton
Introduction by James Colquhoun

Anthony Hamilton served as a Sergeant in the 43rd Regiment of Foot, later the Oxford and Buckinghamshire Light Infantry. He fought at Vimiero and took part in the retreat to Corunna, vividly describing the appalling conditions and the breakdown of the morale of the British Army. He subsequently fought at Talavera, Busaco, the Coa, Sabugal, Fuentes de Oñoro, Salamanca and Vittoria. He also volunteered to take part in the storming parties of the sieges of Ciudad Rodrigo and Badajoz. During these actions, he was wounded three times.

Published privately in New York in 1847, this rare and fascinating account has never before been published in the United Kingdom.

RANDOM SHOTS FROM A RIFLEMAN by Captain John Kincaid
Introduction by Ian Fletcher

Originally published in 1835, this was the author's follow-up to *Adventures in the Rifle Brigade* – and is a collection of highly amusing, entertaining and informative anecdotes set against the background of the Peninsular War and Waterloo campaign.

RECOLLECTIONS OF THE PENINSULA by Moyle Sherer
Introduction by Philip Haythornthwaite

Reissued more than 170 years after its first publication, this is one of the acknowledged classic accounts of the Peninsular War. Moyle Sherer, described by a comrade as 'a gentleman, a scholar, an author and a most zealous soldier', had a keen eye for observation and an ability to describe both the battles – Busaco, Albuera, Arroyo dos Molinos, Vittoria and the Pyrenees – and the emotions he felt at the time with uncommon clarity.

ROUGH NOTES OF SEVEN CAMPAIGNS: in Portugal, Spain, France and America during the Years 1809–1815 by John Spencer Cooper
Introduction by Ian Fletcher

Originally published in 1869, this is one of the most sought-after volumes of Peninsular War reminiscences. A vivid account of the greatest battles and sieges of the war including Talavera, Busaco, Albuera, Ciudad Rodrigo, Badajoz, Vittoria, the Pyrenees, Orthes and Toulouse and the New Orleans campaign of 1815.

ADVENTURES IN THE RIFLE BRIGADE IN THE PENINSULA, FRANCE, AND THE NETHERLANDS FROM 1809–1815 by Captain John Kincaid
Introduction by Ian Fletcher
This is probably the most well-known and most popular of the many memoirs written by the men who served under Wellington in the Peninsular and Waterloo campaigns. The author, Captain John Kincaid, served in the 95th Rifles, the most famous of Wellington's regiments, a regiment which 'was first in the field and last out'. Kincaid fought in most of the great campaigns in the Peninsula between 1809 and 1814 and at Waterloo, in 1815, where he served as adjutant to the 1st Battalion of the Regiment.

THE MILITARY ADVENTURES OF CHARLES O'NEIL by Charles O'Neil
Introduction by Bernard Cornwell
First published in 1851, these are the memoirs of an Irish soldier who served with Wellington's Army during the Peninsular War and the continental campaigns from 1811 to 1815. Almost unknown in the UK, as the author emigrated to America straight after, it includes his eye-witness accounts of the bloody battle of Barossa, the memorable siege of Badajoz – and a graphic description of the battle of Waterloo where he was badly wounded.

MEMOIRS OF THE LATE MAJOR-GENERAL LE MARCHANT by Denis Le Marchant
Introduction by Nicholas Leadbetter   Foreword by Dr David Chandler
Only 93 copies of the memoirs of the founder of what is now the RMA Sandhurst were published by his son Denis in 1812. His death at Salamanca in 1841 meant that Britain was robbed of its most forward-thinking officer. This facsimile edition is enhanced with additional watercolour pictures by Le Marchant himself.

THE JOURNAL OF AN ARMY SURGEON DURING THE PENINSULAR WAR by Charles Boutflower
Introduction by Dr Christopher Ticehurst
A facsimile edition of a rare journal written by an army surgeon who joined the 40th Regiment in Malta in 1801 and subsequently served with it in the West Indies, South America and the Peninsular War. Described by his family 'as a man of great activity and a general favourite with all his acquaintances', he saw action from 1810 to 1813 including Busaco, Ciudad Rodrigo, Badajoz and Salamanca – gaining a well-deserved promotion to Surgeon to the staff of Sir Rowland Hill's Brigade in 1812.

THE DIARY OF A CAVALRY OFFICER 1809-1815 by Lieut-Col William Tomkinson

Introduction by the Marquess of Anglesey

The importance of *The Diary of a Cavalry Officer* for students of the Peninsular War of 1808-14 and of the Waterloo campaign of 1815, as well as its capacity to interest and inform the nonspecialist, is attested to by its scarcity in secondhand bookshops. It is eagerly sought after by both types of reader. There is hardly a serious account of the Peninsular 'running sore' (to use Napoleon's own words), which was a chief reason for his downfall, or of Waterloo, that does not rely in some degree on Tomlinson.

In Spain and Portugal he served with distinction for nearly five gruelling years in the 16th Light Dragoons, later 16th Lancers, one of the best cavalry regiments in the Peninsula.

Some of the important and patently accurate details of many actions in which he took part appear in no other accounts.

But it is chiefly for the penetrating comments on both esoteric and homely, mainly non-military, situations that the general reader will welcome this reprint. As a temporary staff officer Tomkinson was at times close to Wellington and his detailed account of the Iron Duke's working day when not actually in the field is unique.

RECOLLECTIONS OF THE EVENTFUL LIFE OF A SOLDIER by Joseph Donaldson

Introduction by Ian Fletcher

When 16 year-old Joseph Donaldson announced to his parents in 1809 that he had 'gone for a soldier', they were understandably horrified, given the bleak and uncertain prospects facing their beloved son, of whom they had such high hopes. Fortunately for his parents - and, indeed, ourselves - Donaldson returned safe and sound at the end of the Napoleonic Wars and within a few years of his return put pen to paper to record his account of his adventures in that most glorious of British campaigns, the Peninsular War, fought between 1808 and 1814.

The end result of Donaldson's writings was this wonderfully graphic, gripping and often poignant memoir, reproduced here in facsimile for the first time since 1852, along with his two other works, *The War in the Peninsula* and *Scenes and Sketches in Ireland*. In them, Donaldson writes with great skill of his experiences in Portugal, Spain and the south of France, serving with Wellington's army as it fought its way through the Peninsula. His account includes such episodes as Massena's retreat from Portugal, the storming of Ciudad Rodrigo, the storming and sacking of the fortress of Badajoz (a really gripping piece), the battles of Salamanca, Vittoria, the Pyrenees, the invasion of France and the battles of Orthes and Toulouse, all of which Donaldson witnessed as a soldier in the ranks of Sir Thomas Picton's 'Fighting' 3rd Division, the toughest division in Wellington's army.

This is a classic book which ranks amongst the most graphic and enjoyable of the many memoirs of the Peninsular War.

THE PRIVATE JOURNAL OF JUDGE-ADVOCATE LARPENT ATTACHED TO THE HEADQUARTERS OF LORD WELLINGTON DURING THE PENINSULAR WAR, FROM 1812 TO ITS CLOSE

by Francis Seymour Larpent

Introduction by Ian C Robertson

Originally published in 1853, this is a facsimile of the third edition of one of the five contemporary journals, later published without alteration, which Sir Charles Oman has referred to as being an interesting and not always discreet account of his busy life at Head-Quarters, and among the best for hard facts.

In September 1812, the 36 years old Francis Larpent set sail for Lisbon to take up the exacting position of Judge-Advocate-General with the responsibility of reforming and simplifying the disciplinary machinery of courts-martial throughout Wellington's army in the Peninsula, where no form of professional regulation had yet been instituted.

In almost daily contact with Wellington, Larpent's narrative is of especial interest as being written from the point of view of a non-combatant.

This volume is "a must" for all students of the Peninsular War in general and the Duke of Wellington in particular.

For a free catalogue, telephone

Spellmount Publishers on

01580 893730

or write to

The Old Rectory

Staplehurst

Kent TN12 0AZ

United Kingdom

(Facsimile 01580 893731)

(e-mail enquiries@spellmount.com)

(Website www.spellmount.com)